Your Mind
Can Heal
Your Body

MATTHEW MANNING

Your Mind Can Heal Your Body

How your experiences and emotions affect your physical health

PIATKUS

Copyright © 2007 by Matthew Manning

First published in Great Britain in 2007 by
Piatkus Books Ltd
5 Windmill Street, London W1T 2JA
email: info@piatkus.co.uk

The moral right of the author has been asserted

A catalogue record for this book is available from the British Library

ISBN 0 7499 2712 7

175.291
€16.50

Edited by Steve Gove
Text design by Briony Chappell

This book has been printed on paper manufactured with respect for the environment using wood from managed sustainable resources

Data manipulation by
Action Publishing Technology Ltd
Gloucester

Printed and bound in Great Britain by
William Clowes Ltd, Beccles, Suffolk

Contents

Introduction

*People travel to wonder at the height of mountains, at the huge waves
of the sea, at the long courses of rivers, at the vast compass of the
ocean, at the circular motion of the stars; and they pass by themselves
without wondering. (Saint Augustine)*

I have been running a healing centre in Suffolk, England, since the
late 1970s. A high proportion of the people I help have life-
threatening illnesses, and many of my patients are recommended to
see me by their doctors. As a healer, I know that a positive attitude
can contribute to your good health. However, that sort of attitude
can be difficult to maintain if you are faced with a chronic illness or
disability. Such illness produces emotional reactions such as anger,
guilt, sadness, and especially fear. These can add to the distress and
suffering of many of my patients, and may also make their physical
symptoms worse. Sometimes I find that they are ashamed of these
feelings, or don't know how to express them or deal with them.

When the negative feelings become overwhelming, depression
sets in. You might be surprised to learn that depression is a coping
mechanism that humans have evolved as a response to many stressful
life situations, including chronic illness. About 15 per cent of the
population has a chronic medical condition. Western medicine, for

all its brilliance, focuses on cure – but healing is more important. For example, many breast cancer patients are cured by mastectomy, but can continue to suffer emotionally.

I believe that we all have the ability to heal. Like playing a piano, anyone can learn – although some perhaps have greater gifts. This is not to say that with practice you can't develop your healing ability further. People are doing it much more than sometimes they realise. Sometimes it can come in the form of a kind word or deed, occurring in someone else's life just at the moment when they are most receptive to healing. Sometimes it is just being there for someone. Healing is really about caring, concern, love, and a willingness to be of service to others. It is the most simple thing in the world. I've always said that you don't need a degree in medicine or a vast knowledge of Gray's *Anatomy* to be an effective healer. The best healing is achieved when physical and psychological treatments are combined. Furthermore, the earlier such treatment is provided, the greater the benefit. Yet less than 10 per cent of people with chronic illness receive any form of psychological help.

All healing is self-healing

Early in my career as a healer, I was told by a kindly doctor that neither he nor I could make anybody better. All either of us could do, he explained, is to help get the patient's body into optimum condition to heal itself. I know that the people who benefit most from my healing, many of whom I will introduce you to in this book, are those who are willing to help themselves. All healing ultimately comes from within yourself. Your self-healing powers are there, lying within you, waiting to be tapped. You are probably reading this book because you want to help yourself – you have that spark of positive health inside you.

It may come as a surprise to be told that you can take charge of the way you think. We are brought up with the idea that pills and injections from outside can cure physical illness. There ought to be something equally easy to cure emotional hurt and pain, and that is what much of this book is about. Too often we tend to believe that we are the victims of unpleasant thoughts and emotions that just arrive in our head. This can be made worse when what you think or feel is unacceptable to other people who tell you that you shouldn't feel like that – you should 'pull yourself together'. As I will show you, this is not positive thinking or real attitudinal change. It's not always easy to snap out of a negative state of mind and if you try to pull yourself together by pushing aside or repressing unpleasant thoughts, you will probably discover that they emerge again later on, adding to your feelings of helplessness.

If you have suffered a great deal of emotional pain and hurt in the past, you may well be carrying a heavy burden of anger or resentment against those who hurt you. Sometimes these feelings may have turned into anger and hatred against yourself – self-hatred, for example, is a common cause and symptom of depression. The resentment you feel is producing harmful chemicals in your body and is probably affecting your view of the world, but it won't alter the past one little bit.

So how can you think positively, and how does it work? The first thing is to realise that your brain and the thoughts it produces are not your whole self. Your brain can be regarded as an excellent computer into which all kinds of information has been programmed since you were born – by parents, teachers, society, advertising and the media. Because it is *your* brain inside *your* head, it feels like you, and what it thinks feels real and truthful to you. If your computer-brain tells you that you are a worthless person, you'll probably agree with it, and thus add to the store of negative information.

You are not a computer, or a set of conditioned reflexes – you are a human being who was given that computer to serve you. Once you begin to see what is happening, you can start to change the computer programme. I'll be explaining in this book exactly how you can do this to deal with some of the most common, yet negative emotions, which impact our health.

The mind–body connection

I have always been fascinated by the way the body can be influenced or controlled by thought processes and emotions. This fascination stems not only from working with patients for almost 30 years, but also from many remarkable mind–body demonstrations that I have witnessed over the years. In the 1970s, I worked at seminars with a man who had refined the mind–body connection to dramatic effect. His 'tour de force', at the end of his lecture, involved spreading a tarpaulin on the ground, onto which he would deposit a large amount of broken glass. He would invite participants to gather around him and either add more broken glass of their own to the collection, or position the glass in such a way that as many sharp, jagged edges as possible were facing upwards. Once this was done, he would strip off to his boxer shorts and spend a few minutes in a meditative state. Then he would lie down horizontally on his back on the broken glass. While onlookers gasped, and occasionally looked away for fear of the injury he would suffer, he would lie for several minutes taking up whatever position someone suggested.

I saw him perform this feat on numerous occasions, yet he never cut himself – until he was clearing up the glass when the seminar was finished, no longer in his meditative and self-protective frame of mind. As the plasters came out, I knew that the glass was real and potentially dangerous!

The power of the mind over the body is one of the most remarkable aspects of human life. Until fairly recently, it was dismissed as nothing more than mysticism by sceptical Western scientists. However, science is now providing clinical evidence that the mind really can – and does – have an influence over bodily functions. I will be sharing the results of groundbreaking new research throughout this book. Don't just take it from me – it is now being recorded by medical researchers and scientists around the world.

Although most people regard it as a relatively new area of research, the mind–body connection has always been at the heart of medicine. If you believed in a treatment and/or a doctor or therapist, you would certainly *feel* better. Ironically, medical researchers had previously seen the existence of mind–body interactions as a hindrance. Yet the very scientific methods championed by mainstream medicine in the testing of drugs are now providing clear evidence of the extraordinary connections between mind and body. There is a fascinating new branch of medicine called psychoneuroimmunology, which investigates the links between disease and mental well-being. Many of the examples of mind–body interaction that I will discuss in this book have come from new research in this area.

Emotional well-being

People with good emotional health are aware of their thoughts, feelings and behaviour. They have learned healthy ways to cope with stress and problems that are a normal part of life. In one recent test, published in the *Journal of Psychosomatic Medicine* in 2003, scientists led by Professor Sheldon Cohen of Carnegie Mellon University introduced a cold virus to a number of patients and it was found that those with positive emotions were far less likely to go down with a cold. Further experiments have shown that people who feel happy heal more quickly than those who are feeling dispirited.

However, as we will discover in this book, many things that happen in your life can disrupt your emotional health and lead to strong feelings of sadness, anxiety or stress, causing immune system weaknesses that can make you more vulnerable to illness. These may include being made redundant from your job, having a child leave home, getting promoted at work, dealing with the death of a loved one, getting divorced or married, suffering an illness or injury, experiencing financial problems, moving to a new home, or having a baby. 'Good' changes can be just as stressful as 'bad' changes.

Your body responds to the way you think, feel and act. When you are stressed, anxious or upset, your body tries to tell you that something isn't right. If your life is going to be as full as possible, you need to take care of your body's emotional and physical health. We now know that many illnesses can be affected by our good and bad moods, as well as our attitudes. In recent centuries in the West we have lost an appreciation of the symbiotic relationship between the mind and body. We have been too trapped in the narrow confines of rigid physicality.

There are a myriad factors that might lead you to become ill: hereditary, genetic, environmental, dietary and stress factors, emotional issues and psychosocial influences. Your health might be affected by just one of these, or by a combination of them. While I would be wrong to tell you that you can beat illness simply by thinking positively, I nevertheless feel that it is a very important part of any healing programme that works *alongside your medical treatment*.

It is also important to remember that sometimes, no matter how positive you are, no matter how good the medical treatment you receive, no matter what else you do for yourself, an illness can be so aggressive that nothing is going to stand in its way or slow it down. Sometimes, like the best medical treatment, the healing programme that I'm going to share with you may not work. It does not mean that you 'weren't doing it correctly' or that you are 'a failure' – simply that sometimes the biology of a disease is such that the body can still be overpowered. However, I feel that in my work as a professional healer, quality of life is sometimes as important as quantity of life. I know that you will benefit from the ideas, exercises, the inspiring case histories of many of my patients, and the results of a great deal of scientific and medical research that I have drawn from many scientific journals in order to underpin my advice.

This book is all about learning to move towards a more open approach – one that could mean less pain and illness in your life. Most people tend to look at complementary health therapies and techniques for self-healing only when they fall ill. However, you don't have to be ill to find the material in this book useful. I have always thought that we need to move away from the concept of healing only when sickness has established itself and, instead, put the emphasis more firmly on using healing as a means to become more of a complete, whole person before illness has an opportunity to take hold. If at some point it does, you will be better equipped psychologically to deal with it.

Chapter 1
Mind–Body Healing

An essential part of the process of healing has to do with going into the shadow aspects of ourselves – the aspects that, out of fear, we have denied, disowned, or suppressed. (Shakti Gawain)

Although the technology now being used to prove the mind–body connection is highly advanced, it has been known since the beginnings of civilisation that the mind can control or influence the body – witness the extraordinary demonstrations of bodily control by gurus, swamis and Sufis. The ancient Greek philosopher Hippocrates, the founding father of medicine, recognised how important moral and spiritual connections were a part of the process of healing over 2,000 years ago. The connection between mind and body has always been at the centre of Chinese medicine. Medieval Christianity appreciated the relation between the mind and body, but that view disappeared in the seventeenth century.

One morning, so the story goes, the seventeenth-century philosopher and scientist, René Descartes, awoke from a dream, inspired to pursue the study of metaphysics. The culmination of his study was his conclusion that body and mind were separate entities. At that point he and the Roman Catholic Church struck a deal: as a man of science, Descartes would restrict himself to the study of human anatomy, leaving the mind and soul to the care of the church. From that time on, studies of mind and body have for the most part remained distinct and separate fields. Scientists endeavoured to stay within the realm of the observable and strictly quantifiable. Meanwhile, those in the religious life lifted thought, reason and emotion out of the body into the realms of the spiritual.

In an age without anaesthetics, surgery was agonising (as Samuel Pepys recorded in his diary) – and often fatal. The Church's spiritual concerns were of little assistance to those in physical pain. Against this background it was little short of amazing that in 1838 John Elliotson, the revered Professor of Practical Medicine at University College, London, and his protégé James Esdaile, a medical officer for the British East India Company, each reported a large number of surgeries performed painlessly, with hypnosis as the only anaesthetic agent. Against the suspicion of deceit and self-delusion, Esdaile noted the simple fact that his patients referred their family and friends to his service. But he also had data of a harder kind: at a time when surgical mortality was about 40 per cent, Esdaile's death rate was reduced to only about 5 per cent. However, nobody wanted to know, or accept it. Elliotson was expelled from the Royal Medical and Surgical Society and both men were hounded by the establishment.

This short-sightedness continued until the early twentieth century when it was noticed during World War I that soldiers could literally die from fear. The thought of imminent death could sometimes lead to a profound biological breakdown, resulting in death. More significant, however, was the experience of Dr Henry Beecher, a US Army doctor during World War II. On the beaches of Anzio, Italy, morphine for wounded soldiers was in short supply, and Beecher discovered that much of the pain could be controlled by saline injections. Its beneficial influence was based entirely on the power of suggestion and Beecher coined the term 'placebo effect'. His subsequent research showed that up to 35 per cent of a therapeutic response to any medical treatment could be the result of belief. The strength of placebos is now well documented. In 2002, a study published in the *American Journal of Psychiatry* reported that 38 per cent of depressives reported a lasting mood lift having been given (unknown to them) an ineffectual tablet. Even brain scans of these patients showed increased blood flow and electrical activity. The mechanisms involved, even if not completely understood, are so formidable that standard medical research procedure demands separating out their effects from those of the drug.

It is known, from the research of Beecher and others, that medication has an average placebo effect of about 35 per cent – which means that it is your positive thinking and expectation, and not the active drug, working 35 per cent of the healing magic! This effect is not limited solely to drugs – placebo surgery has been found to be effective too. In one study published in the prestigious *New England Journal of Medicine* in 2002, patients with arthritis of the knee were treated just as successfully with a small incision and no further action as those who underwent a proper operation. 'We have shown that the entire driving force behind this billion dollar industry is the placebo effect,' claimed Dr Nelda Wray who led the investigation. In another trial to test the value of a surgical procedure (ligature of an artery in the thorax) to treat angina, the placebo procedure consisted of anaesthetising patients and merely cutting their skin. The fictitiously treated patients showed an 80 per cent improvement (way in excess of the standard placebo response), while those operated on correctly had only a 40 per cent improvement. Seen in this light, maybe there are occasions on which so-called psychic surgery may be effective and explicable.

The power of expectation

Whilst most people will have heard of the placebo effect, which creates a positive effect, relatively few (including some doctors) will have heard of the nocebo, a phrase first coined in 1961, which refers to a negative effect. The nocebo works in several situations: in the one-to-one interaction of doctor and patient, each with their own expectations; in people's general beliefs and expectations outside the therapeutic situation; in the expectations created in groups of people. For example, patients often appear to react to the colour of the pills they receive, regardless of their ingredients. While pink tablets seem to induce a positive reaction, blue tablets are associated with pain.

A simple example of the doctor-to-patient nocebo effect was observed when a group of patients was given sweetened water but told it was an agent that caused vomiting. Eighty per cent of them proceeded to be sick, which may give a clue as to why there are not more nocebo trials! In another experiment, asthmatics inhaled a nebulised saline solution that should have caused them no problems – except that they had been told it was an irritant solution. Almost all of them experienced breathing difficulties and some had full-blown asthma attacks. Later they were given the same saline spray but were told it was a helpful bronco-dilating drug. They immediately recovered. The patients in the study didn't just think their airways were constricting – *they really were.* The bronchial constrictions were caused, or cured, by the patients' expectations alone.

In one controlled study by the British Stomach Cancer Group, 30 per cent of a placebo-treated group lost their hair, and 56 per cent of the same group suffered 'drug-related' nausea or vomiting. While it is understandable that someone may feel sick after taking a sugar pill that they believe to be a toxic chemotherapy drug, the same cannot be said of hair loss. In another study, two-thirds of patients receiving a placebo developed signs of streptomycin toxicity (skin irritation and dermatological allergic reactions) when *believing* they were actually taking the antibiotic. They even experienced high and low frequency hearing loss, a well-known side effect of antibiotic use. If the mind has the ability to create such a negative physical reaction to a placebo, what would happen if it was reversed to a positive response?

Expectation, positive or negative, can be an effective treatment. A placebo or nocebo stimulates the brain in the same way as a drug treatment, even in an illness such as Parkinson's disease. In 2005, Canadian researchers discovered that comparable levels of dopamine, the brain chemical lacking in patients with Parkinson's disease, are released after an injection of a drug *or* a placebo.

The placebo effect is just one way in which science has recently begun to come to accept the importance of the mind's role in healing. Now let me introduce you to some of my patients, who offer practical evidence of the link between mind and body. Their stories are both inspiring and instructional. Maybe you will resonate with their situation and how they learned to use the healing techniques that I will share with you in this book.

Sue's story

I first met Sue in 1994, just six weeks after she had been diagnosed with lung cancer. At the age of 42, and married with a 17-year-old daughter, she had been told that there was no effective medical treatment. The cancer was in the lining of her lung and it had already produced secondary tumours. She had been told that she probably had a year to live and the main tumour was already restricting her breathing. Her doctors had offered her radiotherapy to reduce the swelling, but they explained that it was only palliative to make her more comfortable.

In fact, the palliative radiotherapy eventually affected Sue's windpipe and her ability to eat. It was at this time that I first met her. She had been using my recorded self-healing exercises on a cassette tape before that first healing session. As she explains:

> I hadn't been able to swallow food for a few days. I felt great heat when Matthew laid his hands on my chest. After the healing session I was terribly hungry and we stopped on the way home. I tucked into a huge meal with gusto and had no problems at all. My ability to

swallow had been restored – it was quite remarkable!

The first year came and went. My consultant was so pleased that I was still alive and so well, he jokingly said, 'Keep proving me wrong.'

She did just that and in 2000 was given the 'all-clear'. Final X-rays merely showed scar tissue where the tumour had been. Twelve years later, she is still alive and well. What had happened to prove the original prognosis wrong?

Sue told me that she simply couldn't accept that it was her time to die and she decided to try to fight, directing her anger at the cells that had 'gone wrong'. She found that my self-healing exercises had given her back some hope and helped her to see that she was more than just a victim of a tumour. They led her to a profoundly peaceful space, 'a quietness in all the madness that had become my life'. She imagined pure white dogs with white eyes, sleek and strong, bounding through her body – thousands of them searching for anything that shouldn't be there and devouring it.

Although we may not know *scientifically* how much difference personal efforts of healing, like Sue's, can mean in terms of life extension, it is known *clinically* that if you are engaged in personal healing it can make a transformative difference in your *quality* of life. A growing body of scientific evidence suggests that a strong desire to live, and a continuous movement towards a healthy relationship with life, helps many people in their fight for physical recovery. Conversely, long-term depression, hopelessness and cynicism tend to reduce resilience and increase physical vulnerability. Ultimately all healing is self-healing. A surgeon can carry out a heart bypass operation, but it is your body that performs the healing. The surgeon simply directs and facilitates the process in the same way that I, as a healer, direct and facilitate the regeneration of your body, mind, emotions, and spirit, in a joint effort with you.

Eve's story

Eve, I'm sure, would agree with me. She was devastated when, in 1990, she was diagnosed with a potentially life-threatening tumour in her eye. I chose her as the subject of a healing demonstration at a workshop I was leading in Australia and what happened next was a combination of my healing efforts and then her own. She later wrote:

> The experience was to turn my life around. I had been to the specialist that morning before attending the workshop and the news had been anything but uplifting. Dire warnings were issued about my reluctance and indeed, perhaps bloody-mindedness about having my eye removed and replaced with a coral-like implant. I just couldn't accept that avenue of treatment. Although the predictions were fearful, something in me knew that there had to be a better way. Matthew was to prove that to be so. My eye was looking anything but sexy, half my face was swollen and my eye was painful.

People often ask what they might feel during a healing session and Eve's description is the same as those of most of my patients:

> He placed his hands on my shoulders and the heat was so intense that it caused my body to vibrate. It felt, in a spiritual sense, as if I was being lifted beyond the physical body. I experienced a feeling of floating, being surrounded by intense white light and an all-embracing love. An expansion of the soul is about the only way I can explain it. It was a truly amazing experience. Physically, the swelling went down, my eye became calm, and my nausea had dissipated.

A week later Eve returned to her consultant for a check-up. He was astonished to find that not only had the swelling gone, but the tumour was starting to melt away. He advised her to continue with her healing with me, 'but I can't be seen to be party to this type of treatment,' he said.

Eve consequently decided:

> From now on I was going to be the person who would take care of
> ME. The healing with Matthew has been the catalyst in my life, pulling
> together the whole holistic picture, clearly defining to me that the
> healing journey is with one's own control. The tools are there to
> harness; we have the reins, and the control. It's each and everyone's
> personal journey. The motto of the story is, 'Don't go backwards'. You
> can survive, as I did.

Eve, like Sue, is alive and well 16 years later.

Although Eve was able to describe what she experienced on a
physical level, other people are curious as to the link between
'healing' and 'self-healing'. What happens on other levels when I
treat a patient, and does my input in some way facilitate internal
connections that can lead to a healing outcome? One of my
patients, experienced in meditation, described the experience quite
succinctly: 'If you can't meditate by yourself, Matthew is like some
gentle opening of a huge door that you can't open by yourself.
During a healing session, part of yourself completely closes down –
yet at the same time you remain very alert. The healing experience
is almost like a short-cut to a meditative state and I would most
accurately describe it as a waking dream state.'

The power of your thoughts

Your feelings and emotions are not just an inescapable part of being
human, but also a demonstrable expression of the link between your
mind and body. Medical research has discovered evidence of this
interconnectedness in the waves of hormonal substances known as
endorphins that are triggered by pleasure, and in the racing heart
and surge of stress hormones associated with fear and anger. Your
thoughts, as Sue and Eve discovered, can prompt moods that

become reflected in physiological reactions. These can have an impact, for better or worse, on your health and well-being. People with good emotional health are aware of their thoughts, feelings and behaviour. They have learned healthy ways to cope with stress and the problems that are a normal part of life. They feel good about themselves and have healthy relationships. However, many things that happen in life can disrupt your emotional health and lead to strong feelings of sadness, stress or anxiety. Your body responds to the way you think, feel and act. When you are stressed or upset, your body will try to tell you that something isn't right.

Stress, for example, is one area in which body and mind are strongly linked. Stress and anxiety raise levels of cortisol and adrenalin in the body, which affect the immune system. Cortisol is a hormone related to fear while adrenalin prepares your body to react. Stress has also been shown to trigger other chemicals, which are linked with 'illness type' behaviour including changes in mood and eating and sleeping patterns. Many conditions appear to be exacerbated by stress. Studies have shown, for example, that relapses in people with multiple sclerosis can be associated with stressful events.

But feeling good also affects the immune system. A Californian study proved that laughter is good for you by showing that medical students who had just watched a comedy video had an increased number of virus-fighting T-cells and more vigorous immune-boosting natural killer cells (often known as NK cells) in their systems. Neurotransmitters in the brain can be affected by emotions and, in turn, trigger physical reactions in other parts of the body. There are clear, established links between how we are in ourselves and the health of our bodies. Think of how just a moment's embarrassment can make you blush. Now imagine what long-standing and burning inner feelings might do.

Listen to your body

Angela had been diagnosed with a benign tumour of the pituitary gland in the brain, known as a prolactinoma. Prolactin, a hormone produced by the pituitary gland, is responsible for breast development and controls milk production in nursing mothers; a prolactinoma is made up of a group of prolactin cells that, for some unknown reason, have decided to 'go it alone', to stop taking advice from the pituitary, and simply produce more prolactin than they should. They have bypassed the system, so that it is very difficult to get a message to them to stop doing what they're doing. The secondary effect of over-secretion of prolactin is a cessation of oestrogen production, because it's not a good idea for a breastfeeding mother to get immediately pregnant.

Angela's body was effectively behaving as if she had been pregnant and was now breastfeeding – she was producing milk and experiencing breast pain, and suffering from a huge reduction in oestrogen resulting in no ovulation or periods, and a loss of libido. From a medical point of view, there was a drug that could have alleviated her problem but she would possibly have to take it for the rest of her life. Not liking the idea of taking a drug at all, let alone for so long, Angela had decided to try to treat the prolactinoma holistically: 'I believe that my body needs the chance to find balance itself, and that I should try to discover why I have "created" the tumour in the first place.'

During healing sessions with me, and periods of meditation by herself, Angela reached a remarkable breakthrough of realisation, hearing a message from her body.

> I travelled a very exhausting and emotional journey after my diagnosis – acknowledging, facing and moving through issues that I had buried. The largest of these concerned my apparent 'acceptance' about not having children, my husband having had three from a previous marriage and not wanting any more. Through my work, I discovered

that I was in denial about it and had buried the pain of not being able to have children. Acknowledging the pain to myself and my husband has been incredibly healing. The tumour has proven to be a gift to self-realisation and truth and I know that I've grown because of it.

It is important that, like Angela, you *listen* to your body. Its subtle messages – and less subtle ones such as back pain, repeated bladder infections, ulcers, or a really bad sore throat – could be your body trying to attract your attention. You need to develop ways to tune in to your body's needs, as did Sue and Eve, whether through meditation, visualisation, psychotherapy, or simply talking to a friend. Be open to the messages of your body and its symptoms.

Sometimes a patient tells me about a feeling they have; it might be fear, anger, sadness, longing, love, excitement or something else. If I ask them, 'As you feel [whatever emotion], what are you aware of in your body?' they will probably tell me about the tightness in their jaw, the churning in their stomach, or the ache in their heart.

The first thing for them to do now is to focus their awareness. This is a movement from their unconscious to their conscious and is the beginning of a connection between their emotions, feelings and body. Once this connection has been established, I encourage them to focus on their awareness of what is happening in their body at that moment. Some find the connection with a feeling is too frightening, too threatening, and their defence mechanisms work in such a way that although they are aware of their physical sensations, they don't feel connected with them. They might be able to tell me that 'My stomach feels tight', or 'My shoulders are tense,' or 'My legs feel weak and shaky,' but they cannot identify emotional feelings, like 'I feel scared,' or 'I feel angry,' or 'I feel weak.' For these patients, awareness starts with the physical feeling and they allow their awareness of it to grow and develop later.

Just the process of allowing your awareness of the sensation to exist will sometimes create a connection to the emotion. Often, if you allow the physical sensation to build it will help you to make a connection. You may discover a feeling that your body is expressing or defending – 'I want to hit (I'm angry)' or 'I want to run away (I'm scared)'. When you connect the feelings within yourself, when you can identify the feeling as an expression of an emotion, the next question is 'Who am I saying that to?'

I have watched patients connect their physical feelings with their emotional feelings, move towards an expression of those feelings, and then discover that, although they had been angry with their husband, wife, or partner, it was really their mother or father that they were angry with. Their partner had merely been the present-day target of old wounds from childhood. Perhaps the partner or spouse had been acting as their parent once had and they are now unconsciously replaying their childhood, but with a new cast. With that realisation, the pressure often lifts from the current relationship as they learn that their partner or spouse is not the real person with whom they have an issue.

Similarly, the pressure may be relieved when they realise that they are not as helpless or dependent on their partner as they had been on their parent. They then discover that there are many options open to them that they had never seen before. Their sense of helplessness and powerlessness may drop away as they come to replay the original interaction and learn to develop a renewed sense of power, competence, support and confidence.

Though your body can't actually 'speak' to you, you should still 'listen' to the information it conveys as symptoms of pain, discomfort, fatigue, etc. Your symptoms are signals sent from your organs, glands, immune system and nervous system. They appear as sensations in your body and are usually uncomfortable in some way. Health issues often arise because you need to pay attention to something else in life.

You really *can* improve your health by using signals from your body. Your body constantly responds to physical signals. When you are hungry, you eat. When you are tired, you rest. There are also times when you may choose to ignore these physical cues – have you ever chosen not to go to bed, despite exhaustion, in order to complete a project or meet a deadline? You constantly receive messages from your body that you interpret and respond to, choosing your course of action based on internal and external demands. Your body's feedback monitors measure the various effects that stress and relaxation have on your body, on your heart rate, skin temperature and blood pressure. This pattern of interpretation and response is known as a 'feedback loop'.

It is well known that stress is a major factor in many illnesses. Whenever you are stressed, your body answers back very plainly. When you are aware that your body feels stressed, you can choose an action to relieve the stress. By developing an awareness of your body, your choices for the day-to-day necessities of eating and sleeping will become clearer. When you begin to understand the more subtle signals of your body, you can interpret them better, choosing the most appropriate course of action. It's important to remember that you have the power to change your physiology through your thoughts and through your body.

Finding and relieving physical stress

The following exercise may help you to use both your body and mind to increase your awareness of how you are carrying stress in your body. Have someone read the following questions to you. He or she should read each sentence slowly and should give you plenty of time on each question to make sure you are ready before reading the next question.

Sit or lie down comfortably. Close your eyes, and take a moment to notice where you find tension or anxiety in your body. Don't answer the questions aloud – just think about them.

• *Can you feel tightness in your forehead, jaw or chin?*

- *What about the back of your neck, your shoulders, or anywhere else?*

- *Are you aware of your face flushing, your heart speeding up, your body temperature feeling either hot or cold?*

- *Do you find yourself holding your breath, sighing, scratching yourself a lot, grinding your teeth, or clenching your fist?*

- *Do you feel a knot in your stomach? Or are reactions more subtle?*

- *Do you find that your mind races or goes blank? Do you have trouble concentrating, sleeping or sitting still?*

Make a note of the physical messages. The greater your awareness of the symptoms, the greater is your ability to relieve them. Be aware of any dream-like images that arise, any memories, any scenes of unresolved situations. Listen to your pain or illness as if it were a dream to be interpreted.

This exercise in listening may not produce any startling insights, but don't be surprised if you hear the voice of a small child saying something like: 'I'm tired. I'm lonely. I'm hurt. I'm confused. I'm angry. Somebody take care of me.'

The muscles in your body tend to hold stress in the form of physical tension. But remember, not all muscle tension is undesirable. The muscles tense naturally as part of movement. The difficulty occurs when you accumulate excessive muscle tension and retain it for a long time. As you practise this exercise, you will uncover the centre of the stress and you will increase your ability to relieve the tension in your body and reach an enhanced feeling of relaxation.

Expressing your emotions

We all have different ways of feeling and dealing with emotions depending on the makeup of our body and nervous system, as well as our upbringing and experiences and the culture in which we live. In Mediterranean countries, grief at the loss of a loved one can be openly expressed without censure. In northern European societies, the bereaved may be expected, at least in public, to be 'strong' and to 'bottle up' their tears to spare others discomfort. Our physical constitution also plays a role in how we cope with feelings. Our ability to manage stressful situations can be influenced by individual differences in our body and brain. Both positive and negative emotions have their place in life. It's natural to fear danger, to feel anxious about the unknown, anger at powerlessness, or sadness in the face of loss. Learning to express emotion in a healthy and appropriate way should be a natural part of growing up.

Sometimes emotions can be so strong and confusing that it can help to talk them through with someone – perhaps a good friend or counsellor. Otherwise, feelings that threaten to overwhelm you or that seem socially unacceptable, such as anguish or rage, may be held in check, eventually becoming unconscious. They may then surface in other ways such as illness. Letting yourself cry in an environment in which you feel secure acts as a physical and emotional safety valve. For example, the stress hormone cortisol is released in tears. Problems can occur when one emotion predominates, since you need a palette of emotional colours to deal with life's many predicaments. If you get trapped in a particular mood or feeling, all experiences tend to be interpreted in the light of that mood, thus reinforcing it. If you feel let down and depressed, you tend to view everything pessimistically – you expect the worst and then blame yourself.

Your view of the world has implications for your health. Pessimists tend to lack self-esteem, something that reinforces many other troublesome emotions. Overcoming poor self-esteem provides the 'hardiness' to deal effectively with stressful events. Even quite small shifts in self-perception can bring about profound changes in your life. There is some research suggesting that people who persistently respond to stress by withdrawing and blaming themselves, and who seldom get angry, cry or express other feelings, may be more prone to immune-related diseases. Those who persistently blame others when under pressure may place a different kind of strain on their body.

Three or four days after a really bad argument with your husband, partner or boss, your throat is sore. Although you might think that your shouting hurt your vocal cords, it is more likely that your own anger has boomeranged. Whether or not you won the argument, your strong emotions set the stage for a second battle of which you were completely unaware: the battle between your immune system and a common cold virus. Victory went to the opportunist virus. Your immune system is your first line of defence against foreign invaders. Immune cells travel in your bloodstream throughout your entire body, contacting virtually every cell. Those they recognise, they leave alone. Those they don't recognise, they attack, beating back viruses and bacteria.

It was long believed that our immune system and our brain/nervous system were completely separate. Researchers have recently discovered that the two systems are in constant communication, sending signals back and forth, and your emotions really can affect your immune system. There is scientific evidence to show that by compromising immune function, negative emotions such as fear, anger and guilt can

- accelerate the spread of secondary cancer

- increase vulnerability to viral infections, including common colds and flu

- exacerbate plaque formation in arteries, leading to blood

clotting and heart attack or stroke

- accelerate the onset and course of diabetes

- worsen or trigger an asthma attack

- lead to stomach ulcers

- damage memory

I will look in detail at how to deal with each of these negative emotions – fear, anger and guilt – in the chapters that follow.

Boosting your immune system

Poor emotional health can weaken your body's immune system, making you more likely to get colds and other infections during emotionally difficult times. Moreover, when you are stressed, anxious or upset, you may not take care of your health as you should. Fortunately, there is a lot you can do on your own, without a doctor or drugs, to strengthen your immune system. One of the most powerful immune boosters is having fun, so here is your prescription for laughter and immune-boosting pleasure:

1. **Sleep well.** If you're tired when you wake up in the morning, you're not getting enough quality sleep – or sleep at all – and your immunity is probably compromised. Most people need between six and eight hours a night. Medical researchers at the University of Pittsburgh have found that poor sleep is associated with lower immune system function and numbers of killer cells. These are the part of the immune system that fights viruses or cells that divide too rapidly, as they do in cancer.

2. **Get friendlier.** Socialising with friends and family can boost your spirits and your defences. A study of 276 people, published in 1997 by scientists at Carnegie Mellon University, found that those who had a variety of social relationships were better able to fend off colds and had 20 per cent greater immune function than more introverted people. Researchers now believe that social ties may help us cope with the stresses that lower immunity, as I will show you in the last chapter.

3. **Watch a humorous film**. Medical researchers at the University of California have found that the positive emotions associated with laughter decrease stress hormones and increase certain immune cells while activating others. In one study, men who watched a funny video for an hour had significant increases in gamma interferon, a hormone of the immune system, which activates other components of the system. Another study conducted at the Loma Linda Unversity School of Medicine in California found that when asked to narrate a stressful film in a humorous manner, people who don't typically cope using humour and those who tended to use humour as a coping strategy showed equally positive benefits. Both groups had fewer signs of stress when they used humour than when they narrated the film seriously.

4. **Put some culture into your life.** A study published in the *British Medical Journal* in 1996 showed that those who frequented cultural events such as concerts, museum exhibitions, and even football matches, tended to live longer than their stay-at-home counterparts. The key factor could be increased social contact and reduced stress. It could also be music. Researchers at the University of Cleveland have found that people undergoing music therapy have significant increases in levels of immunoglobulin A – antibodies in saliva that defend against infection.

5. **Write about your life.** Keeping a journal may increase your ability to fend off germs, according to studies by psychologist Professor James Pennebaker of the University of Texas. He found that people who wrote about traumatic events for 20 minutes a day three to five times a week had about half as many visits to the doctor as people who didn't write. Their antibody response to bacteria and viruses was more vigorous than that of a control group. Putting it all down on paper may help you see your problems as less stressful so your body doesn't automatically produce stress hormones, such as cortisol.

6. **Get a massage.** In a study conducted by Gail Ironson, professor of psychology and psychiatry at the University of Miami, 20 men with immune systems weakened by the HIV virus received 45-minute massages five days a week for a month. At the end of that time, they had less anxiety and several of their immune functions improved considerably. Their natural killer cells became more efficient and multiplied. Cytoxic T-cells, a type of cell that helps to regulate immune response, also increased.

7. **Look for spirituality in your life.** Medical researchers at Duke University Medical Center recently reported in the *International Journal of Psychiatry* that people who attended religious services once a week or more had lower levels of interleukin-6, an immune system protein linked to some autoimmune diseases, than non-churchgoers.

8. **Learn to visualise.** Visualisation, a relaxation technique that Sue used in her fight against lung cancer, involves allowing images to drift through your mind. (I will say more about visualisation in Chapter 7.) It may also heighten your immune response to disease. Some studies have shown that subjects using visualisation have increased T-cell and white blood cell

count, while in others there was a rise in natural killer cell activity. Listen to a CD or tape that invokes relaxation, perhaps the sound of ocean waves or someone describing the process of relaxation (see Resources).

9. **Be an optimist.** Having a positive outlook when under stress can make you and your immune system feel high. A 1998 study at the University of California found that law students who began their first year optimistic about the experience had more helper T-cells after six months. These can amplify the immune response. The researchers concluded that a person's outlook and mood when stressed might affect responses to common immune challenges such as exposure to cold viruses. (Chapter 3 deals with optimism in more detail.)

10. **Exercise each day.** Daily vigorous exercise such as walking can bolster your resistance to disease. At least three separate studies have shown that women who walked fast enough to boost their heart rate for 30 to 45 minutes five days a week for 12 weeks had an increased number of immune cells in their bodies for several hours afterwards. But don't overdo it. In high intensity exercise of more than an hour, hormones are released that can suppress the immune system for up to 24 hours.

Bruce's story

Bruce's case illustrates the difference attitude can make. Bruce was diagnosed with a tumour in his bile duct. He admitted without reservation that he is exactly the type of person to whom alternative therapies at one time seemed irrelevant. But that, he said, was before his world was turned around by his diagnosis. The tumour was growing steadily and he had no choice but to have the left lobe of his liver removed, together with his gall bladder and the bile duct itself. He was given just a 25 per cent chance of surviving the eight-hour operation required to remove the most affected parts of his body. But, despite the relative success of the surgery, he was made very aware that there was no chemotherapy or other treatment which could prove effective on his particular cancer.

Instead, his surgery had been regarded as 'non-curative', meaning that some cancer cells had been left in his body. In all probability, due to the aggressive nature of his cancer, those cells would then spread very quickly. In the face of this poor prognosis, Bruce decided to look at other ways of helping himself. 'I decided I wasn't about to sit down and die from this cancer,' he said. 'I'd done a lot of reading while I'd been confined to the hospital, and it had opened my mind to the different approaches people can take.' It was the ultimate start on a life to 'living with cancer rather than dying from it'.

Having attended the Bristol Cancer Help Centre (see Resources), he changed his diet and, to reduce stress, commenced a daily ritual of meditation. He also sought out my help.

> I'm not really the sort of person who would ever have thought about meditating or seeing a healer before getting ill, but I decided it was up to me to do what I could to help myself. Whenever I'm faced with a cynical person these days, I tell them: 'If you're put in a corner, you'll try absolutely anything.' Right from the start, Matthew told me that there could be no promises, and he always made it clear that he's not an alternative to the medical treatment but that he might be able to help alongside it.
>
> In each session he would place his hands over me and it would be all very quiet and restful. I remember in the early days how his hands would feel incredibly hot – like a hot-water bottle – but that seemed to lessen as the sessions continued. All I can tell anyone is that it made a huge difference to how I felt emotionally and physically.
>
> Alongside seeing Matthew, I was sticking to the diet and meditating every morning. I felt I was doing something to help myself and, yes, I believe it's had an effect.

Bruce has now had another scan to see whether the rogue cells are advancing. To his surprise – and delight – there is no indication of growth or spread.

> That's certainly not what the doctors were expecting. They'd made me fully aware of a very bleak prognosis but, right now, I feel fantastic. I'm back at work and there seem to be no medical signs of my health deteriorating.
>
> Yes, you could put it down to a fluke or something else, but I adamantly believe that the healing, change in diet and meditation have all worked together to give me a far greater chance.

Bruce continues to meditate daily for one hour, starting at 6 a.m. He says practices like this have changed his outlook, making him feel brighter – and healthier.

> I can't say that merely meditating has managed to reduce my cancer, but I do know that I feel a lot calmer. That alone must be good for my health, because we all know that the mind and body are affected by each other. In the early days I would be thinking about the cancer all the time, but now, because of the changes I have made, I can honestly say that I don't have much cause to think about it.
>
> I do feel 100 per cent. There's no telling whether that will change but I'm doing everything in my power to encourage the body to be well – at the same time as enjoying every day that comes.

There is an unforeseen postscript to this tale – exactly a year ago Bruce's wife, Jan, was diagnosed with cancer after the changed appearance of one breast led her to be concerned. She says:

> I went to the GP about it and, within three weeks, I had had a mastectomy. Having watched Bruce go through what he did, one of the first calls I made was to Matthew, for some healing before the surgery. Like Bruce, I can't put recovering as quickly as I did down to

one thing – but I was released within 24 hours instead of the usual four to five days in hospital.

Sue, Eve, Angela and Bruce, when diagnosed with serious and possibly life-threatening illness, all decided to try to increase their chances of recovery by using mind–body healing techniques. They discovered ways to cope with their predicaments, learned to work through emotions such as fear and anger, and found the healing benefits of optimism and guided imagery. In the chapters that follow, I will introduce you to some of my other patients who found similar benefits – and to the medical researchers and scientists who have been able to demonstrate the same effects in controlled studies around the world.

Chapter 2

How Are You Coping?

Not everything that is faced can be changed, but nothing can be changed until it is faced. (James Baldwin, writer)

You have just been told that you or a loved one have a major illness, and your world has come to a standstill. Although you did not choose to have this happen, you can choose how you are going to cope. Pain and tiredness may become a frequent part of your day. Physical changes caused by the disease may affect your appearance, diminishing your positive self-image. When you don't feel good about yourself, you may prefer isolation and withdraw from friends. Chronic illness can influence your ability to function at work, potentially leading to financial difficulties. As your life changes, you may feel a loss of control and anxiety about what lies ahead. Stress can build, influencing how you feel about life. Prolonged stress can lead to frustration, anger, hopelessness, and at times, depression. The person with the illness is not the only one affected – family members are also influenced by the persistent health changes of a loved one.

This is a common situation for many people when they first visit me. I believe that the most important step they can make is to take action, as early as possible, to enable them to understand and deal with the effects of a chronic illness. Learning to cope helps to maintain a positive physical, emotional and spiritual outlook on life. With my help, David, one of my patients, quickly designed strategies to help him regain a sense of control over his life – and improve his quality of life.

David had been diagnosed with two tumours on his prostate gland. Scans showed that the cancer had already spread to nearby lymph nodes. Although he was offered hormone treatment, this would not be a cure. Like so many of my patients – whether they have been diagnosed with multiple sclerosis, arthritis, or any chronic illness – he felt stunned and desolate. At first, he felt he was in a situation over which he had little or no control. In the past, if he had an illness like flu or bronchitis, he knew he would be feeling better and functioning normally within a week or so. This time the situation was very different. The disease might never go away and might disrupt his lifestyle in many different ways. He knew that he would have to make major changes and find ways to help himself and his family to cope. When I first met him he was eager to make changes, in order to possibly save his life. He had compiled a list of what he called 'stressors' and 'stress signals'. His stressors were:

• prostate cancer – a chronic illness

• uncertainty about his future

• unpredictability of his disease

• possible financial difficulties if he was unable to work fully

These were in turn causing physical reactions in the form of stress signals that he listed as:

• body aches

• pain

- anxiety

- irritability

- disturbed sleep

- fatigue

- tension

He felt that his healing sessions with me, by helping his physical condition, were also beneficial in helping his stress levels. He found that he was becoming very much more positive: 'I *knew* that I was going to win the battle. This feeling stayed with me and grew stronger than ever.'

However, it wasn't all down to my work with him. He had also set about adopting what he called 'a new regime'. He realised that he urgently needed to reduce stress in his life. He and his wife sold their large house and bought somewhere smaller so as to reduce financial worries. He greatly reduced his working hours in order to spend more time on exercise, yoga, visits to the gym, and pastimes that made him happy. He learned to meditate and visualise, and read as many books as he could find about other people who had helped themselves in similar situations. David's next scan showed that after nine months of lifestyle change, the prostate tumours were dramatically reduced and the infected lymph node was clear. This news gave him a huge boost – he now knew that by taking responsibility for his own life, learning to be more positive, and being prepared to make change, things were going his way.

Different people have different ways of coping with the emotional rollercoaster of illness, but you may find the following checklist helpful in determining how well you are doing. Choose the answer that best matches your thoughts or experiences:

The Coping Scale

Yes No

1. ◯ ◯   I look for more information when problems arise or I get bad news.

2. ◯ ◯   I talk with others and share my concerns when I meet a problem.

3. ◯ ◯   I try to see the humour in a difficult situation.

4. ◯ ◯   On some days, I try not to think about my illness.

5. ◯ ◯   I keep myself busy to distract myself from being ill.

6. ◯ ◯   If reliable information shows that I need to change my treatment, I do it at once.

7. ◯ ◯   Illness has made me re-examine my life, but there are still people and activities I enjoy.

8. ◯ ◯   I think this illness is probably my fate. What's the point in fighting?

9. ◯ ◯   When I'm upset, a drink helps to calm me down.

10. ◯ ◯   I wish people would leave me alone.

11. ◯ ◯   No matter what I do, I can't sleep.

12. ◯ ◯   I can't help thinking that I must have done something bad to deserve this.

13. ◯ ◯   Being ill is bad enough, but to make matters worse no one knows how to take care of me.

The more 'Yes' boxes you ticked for questions 1 to 7, the more you are already using helpful coping skills. If you ticked any of the 'Yes' boxes for questions 8 to 13, you are using common ways of coping with the emotional issues of illness – but unfortunately, they are not the healthiest ways to cope. Sometimes they can drive people away from you just when you need them most. When anger, hopelessness, withdrawal and other negative emotions last longer than a couple of weeks, it can be a sign of serious anxiety or depression. However, the more times you ticked 'No' to questions 8 to 13, the better you are at problem solving and keeping an open line of communication with family, friends and others who are trying to help you.

Medical scientists, as well as people like David, are finding growing evidence that one's coping mechanisms can influence the progress of many diseases. For example, a nine-year study published in 2005 in *Psychiatric Times* has shown that the degree of concealment of gay identity in patients who are HIV positive was strongly linked with more rapid progression to AIDS diagnosis and a faster time to AIDS-related death. There was a clear relationship between disease progression, poor coping and the stress of concealing sexual orientation.

Researchers from the University of Kent published interesting findings in the *British Journal of Health Psychology* in 2002 after interviewing over 200 patients with irritable bowel syndrome (IBS). They found that if sufferers believe their IBS is due to an external factor, such as a virus, and that it can be controlled, they cope well. But if they believe it is caused by psychological factors, they are less likely to cope. Patients were asked about their symptoms and what they believed about the causes and severity of the disorder. They were also asked to what extent they believed their IBS could be controlled or cured, how they coped with it and how anxious or depressed they were. It was found that those who believed their IBS could be controlled or cured were likely to accept it and have a better quality of life. Those who thought IBS was a very serious illness with potentially serious consequences suffered more anxiety and depression, and had a lower quality of life.

Dealing with bad news

If you are given bad news, are traumatised, or are in pain, you may find yourself going into a spontaneous state of self-hypnosis. For example, you might hear the word 'cancer' and not consciously remember anything after that. This is a good reason to take a tape recorder or have someone else go with you to the doctor. (I often adopt the same approach when people first come to me: 'Two pairs of ears are always better than one,' I tell them.) If you are in this state, you may also be highly suggestible, so the next words spoken by the doctor are very important. If certain phrases from doctors or nurses keep repeating in your head (for example 'This is the worst case of . . . I've ever seen'), you will probably benefit from talking to a trained healthcare support person.

You may even find yourself so afraid that you revert to a childlike state, looking to others to make decisions for you. One of my patients recently was so traumatised by everything happening around her after she had been diagnosed with cancer that she had her daughter make every arrangement and appointment for her. She didn't even want to know until the day of an appointment that she had a hospital visit. It was her way of coping without worrying for days or weeks ahead and, for her, it worked perfectly to reduce stress levels. You might find, if you adopt this strategy, that when you are feeling more yourself you are better able to make your own decisions. I would suggest that, unless it is an emergency situation, you try not to make any immediate decisions in a doctor's office. Give yourself time to reflect in a different setting.

Similarly, like many of my patients, you may have been too overcome to think about what further information you wanted. Do not be afraid of asking for an extra appointment, and make a list of questions. Send the list to your doctor's surgery when you make the appointment, or give it to one of the nursing team. Doctors are trying their best in a difficult environment, and letting your doctor know in advance what you want to know can help her decide whether to call you instead, or adjust how much time she will need with you. Suddenly producing a list of questions during your visit can sometimes irritate doctors, not because they don't want to talk to you, but because they are often behind schedule and don't know if you have two or twenty things to discuss.

Some doctors feel uncomfortable giving bad news, and this awkwardness can translate into the appearance of being brusque or unfeeling. They may shut themselves off from feelings because the situation is also painful to them. Do not let your dismay at this attitude interfere with taking care of what you need to do for yourself. Don't dwell on it. If necessary, find another doctor, or find the support you need elsewhere.

Stress and the immune system

How we cope can directly affect our immune system, and therefore possibly our recovery from illness. Medical researchers have discovered that it is our inability to cope with stress, rather than the stressful event itself, that is most damaging to our immune system. Natural killer cells are a type of white blood cell that attacks viral or cancerous cells. They are always ready to recognise and attack an aberrant or infected cell. This becomes very important in the prevention of cancer, and scientists have measured variations in natural killer cell activity based on stress and coping. One study conducted at Harvard Medical School questioned subjects about stressful events in their life and how they coped. Blood samples were then taken and natural killer cell activity measured. The subjects were sorted into four equal-sized groups according to their stress level and their level of coping with it.

Group	Natural Killer Cell Activity
Good coping (high stress/low symptoms)	22.5
Lucky (low stress/low symptoms)	15.1
Neurotic (low stress/high symptoms)	10.6
Bad coping (high stress/high symptoms)	7.5

The results of this fascinating study show clearly that if you have good coping skills, the activity of your natural killer cells is dramatically affected. Subjects with the worst coping skills had the lowest level of natural killer cell activity. That same immune marker was *trebled* in those who had good coping skills.

Some of my patients are very sick children, brought to me by their parents. I never cease to admire the enormous time, strength and dedication that these parents devote to their child, often when they are under enormous psychological and emotional stress themselves. It is not surprising that they seem to suffer more than their fair share of colds, flu and viral infections. Chronic stress does not only make you more vulnerable to catching illnesses. It can also impair your immune system's ability, for example, to respond to the anti-inflammatory signals triggered by certain hormones, possibly altering the course of an inflammatory disease.

To examine what happens to people's immune systems during prolonged stressful situations, researchers at Washington University compared 25 healthy parents whose children were undergoing treatment for paediatric cancer with 25 healthy parents whose children were healthy. All the parents had a blood test at the initial session and saliva samples were taken intermittently over two days.

Parents of cancer patients, understandably, reported more psychological distress than parents with healthy children. According to the study, blood tests showed that the parents of the sick children were found to have a markedly reduced glucocorticoid sensitivity compared to parents of the healthy children. Glucocorticoid, a steroid hormone that affects the functioning of the reproductive organs, also has anti-inflammatory capabilities in the body. In addition it is responsible for turning off the production of cytokines, small protein molecules that are the core of communication between immune system cells, and between these cells and cells of other tissue types. In theory, this could have made the parents more vulnerable to illnesses themselves.

The researchers found that good coping mechanisms reduced the immunological consequences of caring for a child with cancer. In particular, they discovered that social support helped the parents deal with the economic, work and family disruptions caused by the disease and its treatment. There is, they concluded, 'a novel mechanism' through which psychological stress can influence the onset and/or progression of conditions that involve excessive inflammation like allergic, autoimmune, cardiovascular, infectious and rheumatologic illnesses. Again, as with the Harvard Medical School study, it is clear that good coping mechanisms really do help to fight illness.

Of course, some people I work with have wonderful coping skills which are sadly not sufficient to slow down the progress of disease. However, it is also very clear that those of my patients who have the poorest coping skills are usually those who deteriorate and succumb to illness most rapidly. Sometimes a husband brings his wife to me for healing but does not want to join us for the session. I always hope that when she leaves me, she will be more confident, inspired and relaxed. That in itself will help the healing process I hope to start with her. Unfortunately, sometimes during the journey home, the husband will start talking about how someone else they knew had the same illness. My patient will remember them – and how they later died. Unwittingly, the husband has begun an undermining process that may well make it more difficult for his wife to cope. For that reason, I always prefer that both partners join in the healing session. Living with illness brings very different stresses to each party and if the patient's husband or wife finds relaxation by being with us, he or she will also cope better with the predicament.

Different ways to cope

Much current research suggests that unpredictability and feelings of hopelessness or helplessness can lead to reduced immunity and on to illness. Whether stress produces illness is closely tied to your sense of vulnerability as well as your perceived ability to cope with the situation. How well you cope depends on such factors as your overall health. If you are healthy and energetic, you will be better able to manage external and internal demands. Your ability to cope with change or stress will be improved if you believe that you can successfully bring about desired consequences. Personal relationships can be an important source of stress, yet conversely, having social support, for instance being loved and valued, is also a coping mechanism. I will have more to say about this in Chapter 9.

Serious illness is an experience like no other. It leaves no aspect of your life untouched and can create uncertainty, self-doubt, losses and limitations, adjustment, and a lot of hard work. Illness can change the way you see yourself and alter your perceptions of the world around you. You might find that you are mourning the loss of life as it was, and then learn to create a 'new normal'. You may have to accept that life is not the way it was, and that perhaps this change is permanent. The keys to coping are within you, but are sometimes difficult to find. You may face chronic illness first as an overwhelming difficulty, and then as something that has to be endured. Over time you learn to make the best of what you have, but drawing on newly developed strengths and coping mechanisms, you find a new way to navigate through life.

Despite the obstacles you might encounter, you can find help. Education provides new information about illness and treatment options. Support helps us to face our fears and concerns. Hope and humour can help you to survive, to continue to put one foot in front of the other, and even to laugh. Learning to adapt and cope is perhaps the greatest challenge we will ever face, but here are some of my suggestions, endorsed by my patients:

Accept responsibility

It's your life and no one can live it for you. Family and friends may be able to help, but the responsibility must come from you. Victor, who lives with Parkinson's disease says, 'For me, a dynamic coping mechanism is acceptance. That is to say, whatever the condition, whatever the circumstance, accept it with gratitude. Difficult? It is as difficult as unclenching your fist – letting go and saying "Thank you".' Val, who suffers from a rare blood disease, says this isn't at first as easy as it sounds: 'Family and friends will want to take charge in order to help, and sometimes you have to be firm and say "Thank you – but I need to do it my way." I found the ultimate decision on treatment, having listened to consultants, needed to be mine. This gave me a feeling of control.'

Be objective

Take a step back and look at your situation. If you can think of someone you admire, try to imagine what they would do in your situation – and then do it. Try also to look at yourself through their eyes. You may find you have strengths that others can see and you can't. Emily, who has spent over six years living with a potentially life-threatening illness, explained that she had found it very hard to be objective. 'I found it very helpful to think about how my father, who died before I was diagnosed with this illness, would have coped and how he would have dealt with the situation by using relaxation techniques.'

Know your strengths and weaknesses

Be honest and kind with yourself. Vicky was diagnosed at the age of 32 with an autoimmune disease that had attacked her muscles. She had left hospital in a wheelchair, too weak to either stand up or dress herself. 'When I was first diagnosed, one of the most painful things was a feeling of being set apart, isolated, different, not like the others. Now my greatest joy is a sense of connection with other people. I discovered that this is probably the only thing that can't be taken away from me. The love that I feel is so much greater than anything I might have lost. I don't focus on a future I couldn't possibly predict. I don't focus on the state of my body, because when I do I feel bad.' Emily found that her illness had forced her to be really honest with herself for the first time in her life. 'I found counselling sessions helpful to combat falling into a pit of depression and anxiety about an uncertain future and declining health. These sessions have helped me to know myself, accept some things, change certain things and also to be less hard on myself.'

Don't try to cope alone

If and when the time comes, turn to friends and family for support. Val says, 'I found it good to have people around, unless I was really tired, because I often put on an act for their benefit and the act helped me!' Anne, who suffers from multiple sclerosis, found it easier to cope with disability when she began asking for what she wants or needs, although it was something she had to learn to do. 'Be specific when making requests,' she says. 'Educate others about your illness. Respond assertively to insensitive comments from others. Encourage positive relationships and weed out any negative ones. Communicate your appreciation to helpful friends and family members. Touch, hug, love, laugh.'

Try to remain positive

The answer you are looking for may not be apparent or easy, but keeping an upbeat frame of mind will make anything easier to deal with. For many people who live with illness, this can be extremely hard and they often imagine the worst. However, relaxation and affirmations of feeling well can be a useful coping mechanism. Dot, who has secondary breast cancer, says, 'Of course I get days when I am "down" but they are more easily overcome when I can draw on the positivity and – dare I say – optimism I feel most of the time. I am fortunate to be well cared for with a massive support system, but I feel such love and healing around me which is a terrific comfort.'

Geoff, when diagnosed with a sarcoma, said, 'My initial reaction was one of disbelief and despair. My next reaction was to tell myself this situation could be overcome. I've always tried to look for the positive but my circumstances now required a great deal of positive thinking, however difficult this was going to be. I adopted the mantra, "every day and in every way I am getting better and better". I also refuse to accept that I am suffering from cancer – I prefer the phrase "recovering from cancer".'

Terry, another of my patients living with cancer, echoes what many others say: 'While the positive approach is evidently so powerful in helping you feel good, enjoy yourself to the full and stay as well as possible (it absolutely does work!), it's not always easy to "keep it up". Little setbacks (related to the disease or otherwise) can more easily knock you back and you quickly see the dangers, risks and negative effects – it could be all too easy to start down the slippery slope. When this happens, you just have to recognise why you feel bad and force yourself back to the positive mood.'

Be realistic

You are not superhuman. There will be things you can do and things you can't. David explained that on being diagnosed with cancer, 'I would be "selfish" and where possible spend more time trying to do the things that I most enjoyed, such as painting, drawing, printmaking, writing to friends, visiting the pub, holidays and so on. I decided to enjoy the garden but to do little work in it

– we now employ a gardener!' Another of my patients found it was important to 'tell others what I need and want. I'd get worn down if I tried to always live up to what others expected of me. I realised that family and friends don't always know that I want thirty minutes by myself or a nap in the afternoon. I had to identify my needs and express them to those around me.'

Emily also realised that she had always tried to do everything – sometimes at the expense of her own well-being. 'I'm now very careful about how much I take on and try to make plans with gaps and not too many over-commitments. My feelings of wanting to please everyone and not let anyone down have had to be adjusted, but good friends understand that it is not possible to do everything. Quite often the housework has to slide – if I don't have the energy, I let it go.'

Dennis, diagnosed with Parkinson's disease, found that being realistic was a very important aspect of coping with long-term illness: 'Treat yourself, don't beat yourself for not being able to do what you used to do. You are ill and you should make allowances for your changed circumstances. I now work from home whenever possible and although I still feel guilty about this, I have decided to do what is best for me.'

Accept you cannot always be in control

Sometimes the only way to cope is to withdraw from the problem, relax and deal with it later. 'This is especially true after visiting the hospital clinic,' says another patient. 'Everyone seems much worse than me. When I get home it is important for me to relax and forget about it until next time. I try not to think about the illness if I can. If I start getting concerned, I'll go for a walk or create something in my studio. The more creative work I do, the better I feel.' Emily had an interesting insight into loss of control. 'I think the lack of control that I feel in the face of illness is very hard. I've found myself manically tidying and organising and cleaning – which I think is an attempt to keep everything else under control. Again, my counselling sessions have allowed me to explore my fears so that I can get on with my life, trying to relax and enjoy it.'

Relax

Things that give you pleasure are the nourishment you need to get you through difficult times. David found that deep breathing has been the most effective form of relaxation. 'I try to do it every day for about ten minutes. I'll take a very deep breath and imagine I am inhaling a healing power. Then I will breathe it out, this time imagining that I'm breathing out the cancer. If I wake up in the night and cannot get back to sleep, I'll do the deep breathing and I can almost guarantee that I'll be asleep in a minute or two.'

Be open to change

Be willing to try something new if what you've been doing no longer works. Clare, who lives with fibromyalgia, says, 'Sometimes it's hard to remember that being ill doesn't mean you are no longer "you". It just means that you are growing and changing and experiencing life. Change can be a good thing.' Terry's wife, Christine, found that she had to learn to adapt from being a forward planner – always well prepared and in control – to being unable to plan anything even a day ahead. 'I've had to learn to live much more in the moment and to be much more adaptable,' she says.

Take one step at a time

Approach each problem in stages. Start small, and then progress. So many of my patients have found this one of the most useful coping mechanisms. Projecting endlessly into the future is fruitless and exhausting – all any of us have is today. 'I try to divide complex tasks into a series of very small steps,' says Brian, who suffers from multiple sclerosis. 'I pace myself in taking each step one at a time – sometimes literally! I don't place any time limit on accomplishing a particular task unless it's absolutely necessary. I've learned not to push, and to take frequent rest breaks. I also only attempt tasks at what I consider to be my most cognitive times of the day and I avoid performing cognitive tasks when I'm "brain-dead".'

Learn to laugh

Having a sense of humour brings relief – and often a new perspective. It's not always so easy – a number of people have told me that they've experienced a total 'sense of humour failure' and have had, like Dot, to work at having a good laugh. She says that she and her family found this particularly helpful: 'We have taken time out of our hectic schedules to really talk, *laugh*, and remind ourselves of things the children did when they were younger. We've had such fun doing it and I've been able to reassure them, well in advance, that death holds no fear for me. I cherish the closeness that humour and laughter has brought us all.' David also found humour – 'tumour humour' as it's known – and laughter to be a useful coping tool: 'I found that I started making jokes about my cancer. Some people may have felt uncomfortable, but my best friends just laughed along with me!'

Terry told me that an American friend decided from the beginning that humour was the best medicine and has faithfully sent a funny card with wacky comments every single week since then. It's a philosophy that he has found extremely helpful: 'As so many say, humour and a good laugh are key to keeping and staying well and enjoying yourself – including laughing at and with yourself and the situation. Christine and I joke about it and can sometimes be quite irreverent. Our son recently rang to ask if I'd still be alive in November for an important babysit – this all seems natural and helps to keep the illness in its place!'

Dennis says, 'I've always had a warped sense of humour and my Parkinson's has just made it worse. If you can laugh, then you're on the right track. Try to see the funny side of situations – good or bad – and you'll soon be spilling your drink over the best of them!' Sometimes dark humour is essential to survive in a dangerous situation. Laughter relieves emotional tension, relaxes your muscles and imitates an aerobic workout through cardiovascular stimulation. It triggers your endorphin system, which helps to relieve pain and enhance your immune system.

Reward yourself

Living with a chronic illness can be hard – you deserve a reward. 'I found frequent holidays help,' says another of my patients. 'Not necessarily two weeks in an expensive resort. Perhaps a weekend in a luxurious hotel – you can't beat a bit of pampering! My wife's comment was, "Let's spend our children's inheritance".' Emily has also found it crucial to indulge herself: 'I have a massage or reflexology whenever I can. I don't feel these are an indulgence – I feel they are really essential in coping with illness – pampering my brave body.'

Learn to say 'no'

This is one time when you really should be doing what you want. Remember the old saying: 'In saying "yes" to someone else, you may be saying "no" to yourself.' As with many of my patients, Dennis found this particularly helpful if not always easy. 'Learning to say "no" can be difficult. If you have not emotionally accepted your plight there is a tendency to say "yes" too quickly, perhaps before you have considered all aspects of how acceptance may or may not affect you. Sometimes I feel guilty if I turn down an invitation from family or friends, but I now know I need more "me" time.'

I can help you cope

After working as a healer for almost 30 years, I would also add the following guidelines as very useful tips for the person who is ill to ask of those around them:

1. Be honest with me. Telling me the truth will ease tension for both of us.

2. Listen to me, even if I repeat myself.

3. Remember that a physical illness can affect my mind, emotions and spirit, too.

4. Volunteer your help: prepare food for my family, offer transport, make phone calls, look after my children, organise others to help.

5. Send cards and letters. Make short visits frequently.

6. Remember that sometimes I need to be alone. Respect my need for privacy.

7. Bring me your emotional support. Talk about the future with me. Hope keeps me going.

8. Words aren't always necessary. Your touch can speak volumes.

9. Don't be afraid to talk about difficult subjects. Ask me how I'm feeling.

10. Encourage me to stay active, but remember my limitations.

11. Learn about my illness. Be aware of any support groups that can help during stressful phases.

12. Keep me informed about the family, the community, the world.

13. Give me your empathy but not your pity. Remember that we all have the same 'human' needs. Showing that you care gives me courage.

14. Don't be afraid to talk about my illness, but don't always talk about it.

15. Accept my negative feelings and fears. It's important for me to talk about them.

16. Cry with me, laugh with me. I need to share this with my friends and loved ones.

17. Pray for me and with me.

Commitment, control and challenge

Learning to live with and cope with an illness can be an enormous challenge. Sometimes there may not be easy solutions to the problems you face. Medical research shows, however, that there are those who not only cope but also continue to grow as people, using certain psychological strengths that anyone can develop.

Your feelings are important. When you are stressed, your body releases chemicals that make you sweat. Your heart rate speeds up and your stomach churns. Prolonged stress is harmful to your health. But what happens if you are happy? Is the opposite true? If you replace the stress in your life with positive thoughts and energy, will you be any healthier? A growing body of scientific evidence is suggesting that it will. The hormones that link your emotions to your physical responses work both ways. Negative, stress-related emotions can contribute to illness, whereas positive emotions suppress the release of stress hormones and can help you to fight illness.

One of the most important and influential researchers to document the link between good health and coping skills is psychologist Suzanne Kobassa. In 1979 she published what was to become a ground-breaking paper, 'Personality and Resistance to Illness', in the *American Journal of Community Psychology*. Her research clearly demonstrated that the difference between those who cope and those who don't – thrive or dive – often depends on three characteristics:

- **Commitment.** Those with a sense of commitment are aware of what they believe in and what goals they have. They are able to articulate these and are willing to change them based on new insights. They live their life in congruence with their goals and beliefs. Basically, they do what they believe and believe in what they do.

- **Control.** This is defined by the ability to realise that there are some things which we have control over, and some things we do not. Those who thrive are able to focus their energy on the things they do have control over rather than wasting time and energy trying to change things they have no control over.

- **Challenge.** This is exemplified by those who possess a certain level of vigour, a willingness to learn and try new things, an ability to work through problems, a knack of finding alternative solutions, and an understanding that 'if I fail in what I do, I have not failed in who I am'.

If you want to have a better sense of control, then you also need to have a good sense of humour. Humour helps you psychologically, emotionally and physiologically. You can maintain your sense of humour by seeking out others who have a sense of humour. You can make yourself do those things which, at the moment you may not feel like doing, but nonetheless, you know you will enjoy.

You can also keep better control by maintaining a better sense of perspective. It is tempting to try to convince yourself and others that the trying times or issues you are facing are catastrophic. Yet, by doing so, you cause yourself to feel powerless to deal with them. You need to ask yourself how awful the current situation is compared to how awful it could be. You have much more control than you might realise – the key is to use it. You can feel as controlled by your own habits, rituals, and routines, as you can by any outside force, yet you have control over these. Either use the control or lose the control.

For a sense of challenge, you need to have one or two special friends in your life with whom you can be perfectly honest and from whom you can get honest feedback. They can help you to learn about yourself and become more self-aware.

Maintaining a sense of challenge includes a willingness to take risks. You need to practise the skill of risk-taking as you do with any other skill. If you do so, you learn that the world will not suddenly end if you are not completely successful. When you do succeed, you realise that the perceived 'danger' is often much greater than the actual danger.

Accept and win

All of your emotions will come and go as you try to cope, but by taking one step at a time you will be able to move to a new state. Learning to cope can sometimes feel perplexing but the following guideline may help you:

$$A+CC+E+P+T = WIN$$

Acknowledge your emotions and losses.
Consider alternatives.
Choose a course of action.
Express yourself. These are some of the ways in which my patients have learned to express themselves:

- talking to a counsellor or friend

- writing or painting, or doing something else creative

- taking time alone to think, feel, contemplate, relax

- enjoying music

- taking a walk

- exerting themselves physically

- doing some gardening

- thinking positive thoughts

Patience. It takes time to heal and recover. Allow yourself plenty of time to recover, and look back to see your progress.

Try something:

- rest and relax

- maintain basic routines if possible

- be active, varying the amount each day according to how you feel

- say 'no' to activities that may tax you emotionally or physically

- be good to yourself

WIN: What you win is a personality capable of *coping*. You will still feel love for what may have been lost, but without the pain.

Chapter 3

Healing and Optimism

Optimism is essential to achievement and is also the foundation of
courage and true progress. (Lloyd Alexander, children's author)

How do you see yourself, your relationships, the world and the
anticipated outcomes of your life? Are you generally optimistic or
pessimistic? How you see life is a component in how it will turn
out for you. Some people expect the worst outcome of any event.
These people are known as pessimists. Their partners often call
them negative and find their attitude draining. Pessimists' attitude to
life can contaminate the feelings of their more positively inclined
partner. As one of my patients put it, 'It's hard to stay happy when
my husband is always negative.' Other people are hopeful and
positively inclined in terms of the outcome of events. They
anticipate success and deal with setbacks as challenges, not evidence
of their ineptitude. These people are known as optimists.

The origins of optimism and pessimism are not altogether known.
There has been research supporting the idea that some genetic
element exists in regard to optimism. It is also safe to assume that
parental pessimism is something that we learn. Some negative views
of life may stem from unfortunate early life experiences over which
you have no control, although there are still many people who had

similar unfortunate events and adopted a hopeful outlook and a positive disposition. Whether pessimism is innate, learned or acquired, it serves you poorly.

Medically, studies have shown that the health of pessimists is seriously compromised. A report in a paper to the American Psychosomatic Society in 1995 showed that pessimism 'was a significant predictor of early mortality among young cancer patients with recurrent cancer'. A study of Harvard University graduates found that, compared to optimistic men, 'pessimistic men had significantly poorer health or were more likely to have died when they were assessed 20–35 years later'. A 2001 report in the journal *Stroke* concluded that patients' attitudes to their stroke are associated with survival. Patients who were pessimistic, feeling hopeless and helpless, did not survive as long as other patients. This was true even when physical factors, such as stroke severity, were accounted for. Other studies did not find a direct correlation between pessimism and health but found that pessimism affected the immune system through increasing the patient's stress level, which impacted on health.

Dr Carol Craig runs Glasgow's Centre for Confidence and Wellbeing, and is passionate about curing Scotland's epidemic of pessimism and low self-esteem. She points to many indicators of pessimism: the Scottish suicide rate is double the English one, and antidepressant prescribing is 40 per cent higher. A new United Nations report says that Scotland is the most violent country in the developed world. Scottish children are among the least confident anywhere, according to the World Health Organization.

Craig believes that the dark, forbidding nature of Calvinist religion is responsible for the dour Scottish psyche: 'We are a culture that encourages feelings of lack of self-worth. We are a culture that goes out of its way to make sure people don't feel good about themselves.' From a young age, Scots are taught humility, modesty and conformity. Scottish humour often pokes fun at those who get 'above their station'.

Craig speculates that the high level of emigration from Scotland has depleted the country of optimists and left too many pessimists behind. Could this be linked to the fact that men in Shettleston, a part of Glasgow, have a life expectancy of 64? (Scottish men, on average, live to 73.) West Scotland is the unhealthiest region in Europe, with high rates of heart disease, strokes, and cancer. In 2005, a team from University College London studied the happiness levels of 216 middle-aged civil servants in a study of risk factors for coronary heart disease. Those who had the most happy moments per day had the lowest level of cortisol, a hormone that can be harmful if produced excessively, and of the chemical plasma fibrinogen, a predictor of heart disease. The happiest men (but not women) also had the lowest heart rates.

Pessimism and relationships

Pessimism often manifests itself as negativity, powerlessness, and a self-defeating attitude. It has been shown that pessimistic people are more likely than optimists to suffer setbacks when bad things happen to them. Pessimists often personalise events and see their bad luck as a sign either that they have failed, or that they are unworthy. This helpless position makes them feel victimised by life. And when they say 'bad things always happen to me', they interfere with their ability to minimise bad outcomes or the impact of unfortunate happenings on them.

The pessimistic view leads the believer to self-centredness, self-hate and futility about control in their life. All three things are difficult to integrate into a healthy relationship. The partner of the pessimist often begins with reassurance, trying to dispel myths about unworthiness and periods of bad luck. In time, the pessimist is seen as unavailable, unapproachable and powerless within the relationship. Pessimists also lose out on fun, adventure, creativity and exploration in life because they always anticipate the worst outcome. They shoot down their partner's suggestions with a list of objections due to potential problems and failures and partners often get discouraged from suggesting anything. They are then left to create their own fun, which creates further distance. If you are pessimistic, consider these points:

- Your view of life is counter-productive for your relationships and your health.

- Living with a pessimist is a challenge. Negativity interferes with intimacy.

- You deserve to have a happy, successful and intimate life.

- You cannot continue to hide behind your personality. 'I can't help it, I was born this way.' You *do* have the power to change your belief system.

- Learning that the glass is actually half full will improve your emotional, physical and spiritual life.

Optimism and realism

It is also important, however, to point out that there are many people who blindly believe and will tell you that if you have unwavering hope, are positive and inspired, and an aggressive fighter of disease, it will help you overcome almost any illness. The implication is that positive thoughts are a cure. While optimism is tremendously important in the healing process, it needs to be tempered with realism.

Positive thinking and optimism can improve some people's lives in numerous ways, but untempered they can cause harm. Sadly, I receive at least a couple of letters each month from women who have been diagnosed with breast cancer but have declined medical treatment on the grounds that it is 'dangerous and invasive'. My response is that so too is their cancer. Invariably they believe, with what I think is misguided optimism, that by changing their diet, meditating, and following alternative therapies they will recover. The evidence for this is pretty much non-existent. If it worked, it would be widely used and integrated into mainstream medicine. An unrealistically optimistic attitude can sometimes prevent people from seeking medical treatment – a decision with which I would never agree. Healing and medicine can, and should, work hand in hand.

Dr Andrew Weil, an American doctor with a foot in both camps, has the best response. He says that the common cause of all cures is in the healing system, whether or not treatment is applied. When treatments work, he says, they do so by activating innate healing mechanisms. Treatment – including drugs and surgery – can facilitate healing and remove obstacles to it, but treatment is not the same thing as healing. Treatment originates outside you, but healing comes from within. Nonetheless, to refuse treatment while waiting for healing can be foolish.

It is important to stress that both optimism and pessimism are attitudes based on belief, not facts. If you choose to engage on a venture, where the early data suggests that the project may not succeed, choosing to abandon the project is not a sign of pessimism any more than continuing with it is necessarily a sign of optimism. It may be related to the interpretation and projection of facts.

There are many people who have never had a positive, optimistic, 'everything will be fine' outlook – and some of them have been my patients. I know that they are not going to adopt such an attitude while being diagnosed with a serious illness, enduring painful and draining treatment, and possible death. Some people cope by being realistic and quietly stoic.

Some patients feel especially hopeless *because* they just can't become optimistic, even though their treatment is going well or has been successful. Because so many self-help books say you must be positive, they feel afraid and worried that they don't have the 'right' attitude. Sadness and fear do not make tumours grow. No one is going to die because they cannot keep a positive attitude. Some therapists and 'healers' are so into positive thinking that they actually blame people for having a brain tumour or cancer. (Just take a look at some of the internet websites to see what I mean.) It is irresponsible and, ultimately, cruel. Cancer cannot be caused or controlled by your optimistic or pessimistic thoughts, although optimism can perhaps help you to cope with growing cells.

What *is* a useful attitude, psychiatrists and doctors say, is to adopt whatever philosophy helps you to stick with your treatment and to acknowledge and express your honest feelings – positive or negative. If at some point it is no longer realistic to hope for a cure, then refocus your hope towards a more realistic goal: maximising your day-to-day quality of life. A number of my patients have said that a life-threatening illness is like rape. Many people find it easier to believe that bad luck hits people who have somehow asked for it – as in rapes blamed on women for wearing provocative clothing or being in the wrong part of town – than to accept that in life very bad things can happen to very good people, for no fair reason. It is great to have a positive attitude if you have any serious illness. At the very least – and this is no small benefit – it is likely to improve your day-to-day quality of life. But if you feel depressed and down, don't feel that you have to keep battling on as if nothing has happened. Sometimes, you may not feel optimistic or courageous – you may just want to curl up in a corner and suck your thumb!

Pessimism among practitioners

Gill was one of my earliest 'star' patients. She had first come to me in 1979 having some years earlier had a mastectomy for breast cancer from which she had completely recovered. She now had secondary lung cancer and had been told that her condition was incurable and that she had only three months to live. She 'knew the situation was pretty bad' and was determined to do everything she could to help herself. She used my self-healing recordings and visited me on a regular basis for healing sessions. 'When it got to Christmas I felt very emotional because I had never expected to live that long. Although I was very positive, deep down I did wonder whether it was going to be my last Christmas. I wanted to get all the family around because I felt it was probably the last one.'

Just over a year later Gill had another scan. When she returned to the hospital for her results, her consultant looked pessimistically at her, her notes, at the scan, and back again to Gill. Finally, he said, 'Well – I've got your scan results. I've got good news and bad news. Which would you like first?'

Having spent over a year working with optimism and positivity, Gill opted to hear the good news first.

'The good news is that we've got your scan results. We've checked every part of you – your lungs, liver, bones and brain. You are completely clear of cancer. We can't see any trace of cancer anywhere. I don't know what you've done.'

Having received the good news, Gill said, 'That's fantastic, isn't it? But if that's the good news, what is the bad news?'

'The bad news is that you must live with the knowledge that, unfortunately, it will eventually return.'

Incensed by his pessimism, Gill did something quite out of character. She got out of her seat, banged her fists down hard on his desk, and shouted 'The hell it will!' That became the motivating factor to keep her going. She told me many times that she was determined to die of something different just to prove him wrong. Eighteen years later, the cancer did recur, and she died in 1997. She had lived for 18 years after being told that she had three months to live. She often said in those years, 'Why could that doctor not have said, "You're in remission – let's hope it lasts."' That would have been the optimistic response, but her consultant chose a pessimistic message instead. What would have happened if Gill had been less positive, optimistic and robust?

Unfortunately, the response that Gill met with from her consultant is still commonplace today, although it is now being more openly addressed by the medical community. In 2002, *The Lancet* published a report entitled 'Cancer doctors could benefit from training in communication skills'. Its authors noted that 'senior doctors working in cancer medicine could benefit from intensive communication skills training to assist the often complex and distressing issues surrounding cancer care'. Another recent report in the *British Medical Journal* states that 'Many studies have found significant positive associations between doctors' communication skills and patients' satisfaction. Several studies clearly show a correlation between effective communication and improved health outcomes.' These were listed as improved emotional health, resolution of symptoms, pain control, and physiological measures such as blood pressure and blood sugar concentration.

Pessimism can be catching, as a remarkable report in the *Southern Medical Journal* demonstrated. Dr Clifford Meador explained how a cancer patient was told, in an echo of Gill's story, that the disease had spread to his liver and he had only a short time to live. The despairing patient died a couple of months later, yet an autopsy revealed that his diagnosis was *incorrect*. He had only a two-centimetre nodule on his liver that was not life-threatening. He had died not of cancer, but of fear. The only thing that could be determined, wrote Dr Meador, was that 'he had died thinking he was dying of cancer, a belief shared by his wife, family, his surgeons, and me, his internist'.

This echoes an anecdote of Denis Granville, Dean of Durham, in 1690, of which Ozzy Osbourne would be proud! 'A French doctor had a patient who was convinced he was possessed by the devil. The doctor called in a priest and a surgeon, meanwhile equipping himself with a bag containing a live bat. The patient was told it would take a small operation to cure him. The priest offered up a prayer, and the surgeon made a slight incision in the man's side. Just as the cut was made, the doctor let the bat fly, crying, "Behold, the devil is gone!" The man believed it and was cured.'

Faith and suggestion – optimistic or pessimistic – have always been at the heart of medicine. If you believe in a treatment and/or a doctor, you will certainly feel better and sometimes get better, even if he has given you a sugar pill or let a bat out of a bag. Remember too the placebo surgery that I described in Chapter 1.

Research into optimism and pessimism

It seems obvious that a pessimistic attitude, where you expect the worst outcome or failure, will make for a less than fulfilling life emotionally. Research confirms that pessimism can also be detrimental to your health. Janice Kiecolt-Glaser and her husband Ronald Glaser have done more research into the mind–body connection than anyone else in the world, having had over 350 papers published in scientific journals. They have discovered that negative emotions and pessimism can intensify a variety of health threats including cardiovascular disease, osteoporosis, arthritis, type 2 diabetes, certain cancers, Alzheimer's disease, and frailty and functional decline. They also contribute to prolonged infection and delayed wound healing.

An American research study conducted at Yale and Miami University tracked the lives of people over 50 for 23 years and found that those who embraced the ageing process lived an average of seven and a half years longer than those who were pessimistic about getting older. Other studies have shown that optimists are not only less likely to die from heart disease, but if they do develop it, recover considerably faster from coronary bypass surgery than their pessimistic counterparts.

Although there are no clear explanations for the health benefits a positive outlook brings, scientists have discovered that there are definite links between optimism, pessimism and the immune system. Professor Christopher Peterson, a psychologist at the University of Michigan, carried out a carefully designed test to determine his students' level of optimism and pessimism – they answered questions about their general health, including how often they went to a doctor. He then followed the health of his students the following year and discovered that the pessimists had twice as many infectious diseases and made twice as many visits to the doctor as the optimists.

Professor Martin Seligman, the godfather of research on optimism and pessimism, found using interviews and blood tests that optimists have better immune activity than pessimists. Numerous other studies have now shown the same thing. Seligman says that optimism is not about ignoring what is real, but becoming aware of your thoughts about why things happen. What is at the heart of optimism is how you explain negative experiences to yourself. When something bad happens to a pessimist, they are likely to get into a thinking pattern that will say something like, 'It's my entire fault. It's permanent. Everything is ruined.' An optimist is likely to say, 'It was bad luck, but it will pass and I'll handle it differently next time because I learn from my experiences.' Optimists feel a greater sense of control over their future – and their health.

A study published in 2002 by the prestigious Mayo Clinic reported that people who expect misfortune and only see the darker side of life experience more pain and don't live as long as those with a more optimistic view. Researchers evaluated results from a personality test taken by participants over 30 years previously and compared them to later mortality rates. The study showed that those who scored high on optimism had a 50 per cent lower risk of premature death than those who scored as more pessimistic. Besides a lowered risk of early death, researchers found other health benefits related to positive attitude. They found that those who scored high on optimism had:

- fewer problems with work or other daily activities because of physical or emotional health issues

- less pain and fewer limitations due to pain

- less interference from physical or emotional problems when engaging in social activities

- increased energy

- more peaceful, happier and calmer feelings.

The researchers involved in the study believed that the results could lead to ways to help pessimistic people change their perceptions and behaviour, and thereby improve their health and perhaps lengthen their lives. They were unable to definitively explain how a pessimistic outlook acts as a risk factor for decreased longevity.

It is known, however, that if you are depressed or pessimistic, certain brain hormones become depleted, creating a chain of biochemical events that cause a slowing down of the immune system. For example, two important cells in our immune system are T-cells and natural killer cells. T-cells recognise invaders, such as viruses, and proliferate to kill off the invaders. Pessimists' T-cells don't multiply as quickly as those of optimists, allowing invaders to get the upper hand. Natural killer cells circulate in the blood and kill whatever they come across that they identify as foreign, such as cancer cells. Pessimists' natural killer cells can identify foreign entities, but they don't destroy them as well as optimists' natural killer cells.

Another study tracking the lives of 238 cancer patients revealed that pessimism in participants under 60 posed a significant risk for mortality. Why? The study's researchers think pessimism might impede the effectiveness of the immune system and suspect that pessimistic patients are less likely to stick to their medical treatment

– patients who believe they are 'doomed' would see little point in treatment.

Findings published by the Mayo Clinic in 2005 also explored a link between a negative outlook and physical health. Participants who scored within the top 25 per cent for pessimistic thinking and anxiety were more likely to develop Parkinson's disease in later life. Even more striking was yet another Mayo Clinic report which revealed that those deemed 'very pessimistic' increased their risk of dementia by 30 per cent. While it is too early to fully understand the role pessimism plays in Parkinson's and dementia, these same researchers – ironically – point to a bright side: negative thought and behaviour patterns that pessimists use to explain personal and life occurrences *can be changed*.

Ways to change your attitude

If pessimism has been your lifelong habit, you can use these tips to learn to cultivate a more upbeat attitude – and it's never too late to start!

- **Notice how your friends feel.** Look at your friends' attitudes. Optimism and pessimism are both contagious states. So to 'catch' optimism, associate as much as possible with positive people.

- **Savour your successes.** We are trained to be modest, but there is no need to belittle your own successes with 'I was just lucky.' Instead, you can say to yourself, 'I worked really hard. I did a good job and I'm proud of myself.' That is the optimistic way of thinking about good events that you brought about by your own efforts.

- **Make the best of hard times.** Some people face a great deal of adversity and still call themselves optimists. Why? When you're an optimist, you also believe 'I can make the most of what I've got.' Sometimes you need to redefine your objectives and let go of an initial expectation. Your basic objective is then to make the most of what you still have.

- **Face facts, but never give up.** Optimism does not mean you are not in touch with hard facts. Be realistic about what has happened in your life. 'Yes, I've had it tough,' 'I was a victim of circumstance there,' 'That was my fault, that wasn't,' 'I did this well.' Then use optimism to resolve it by telling yourself, 'With effort, initiative and good luck, I'll still have things to look forward to.'

- **Distance yourself from your own negative beliefs.** It is essential to realise that your beliefs are just that – beliefs, not facts. We often say spiteful things to ourselves. 'I can't do it. I'm so stupid.' If you think there is some truth to what your inner pessimist is saying, the key is to limit its impact. By putting faults into perspective you will avoid the slippery slope of pessimism – one that creates catastrophe out of insignificant events or details and can wreak havoc on your health.

- **Learn your optimism ABC.** Three things happen in life when you face a difficult or tough situation, and this ABC is a good way to remember the pattern. You respond to **A**dversity with a **B**elief, which determines the **C**onsequence. When you respond to adversity with an optimistic belief, the likely consequence is that you'll feel relaxed and energetic. Compare that to what happens when you respond with a negative, pessimistic belief. It produces an equally negative consequence – you feel worse about yourself.

- **Derail negative thoughts.** Listen to your internal tape carefully, especially during moments of disappointment. If you are personalising events and making sweeping universal and permanent statements, take a moment to stop, breathe, and challenge your thinking. When you become aware of your negative thoughts, you can learn to stop pessimistic thinking. When a persistent negative thought runs repeatedly through your mind try saying 'Cancel', or write down the thought and think it over later. This can stop a bout of pessimism before it starts.

- **Give a little.** If painful circumstances have made you unhappy, doing what you can to help others may give you a more optimistic view. Whether you do volunteer work or simply offer to listen to a friend's troubles, you can find a way to give. There is a real sense of fulfilment in giving that can lift you out of your pain.

- **Get help for depression.** If you are a real pessimist, there is a high chance that you are also fairly depressed. Chronically unhappy people do a running negative commentary on their lives that they are often not aware of. A good cognitive therapist can teach you ways to divert yourself when you get in these moods.

Give optimism a chance

For years social scientists have chosen pessimism over optimism when it comes to studying human nature. So disreputable was optimism that one of the modern era's most influential thinkers, Sigmund Freud, equated optimism with ignorance!

When faced with conflict, people tend to explain life in one of two ways. Martin Seligman has found that when bad things happen, pessimists tend to explain them in permanent, universal and personal terms while optimists explain them as temporary setbacks specific to the immediate situation, and due largely to external causes. Pessimists will tend to think that it will be permanent ('It's going to last forever'). They generalise the problem to their whole life ('It's going to ruin everything') and blame themselves ('It's my fault. If only …'). These habitual ways of thinking can strongly influence our moods, our mental health, even our survival. (However, we shouldn't be too down on pessimists, because in some areas *moderate* pessimism may spell success. They are known to do well in design and safety engineering, technical and cost estimating, contract negotiation, financial control and accounting, business administration, statistics, technical writing, quality control, and personnel and industrial relations management.)

When you have confidence in your ability to think and act positively and optimistically, you can persevere when faced with difficult challenges. The result is that you succeed more often than you fail. You expect more of life and yourself. If you are pessimistic, you are more likely to give up easily, aspire to less, and fail more often – with the result that you get less of what you want. This is also known as self-esteem. It is a necessary condition of well-being. However, it is not the only one. Its presence doesn't make life problem free. Even people with high self-esteem can experience anxiety, depression or fear when overwhelmed by issues they don't know how to cope with.

Healthy self-esteem

I think of self-esteem as the immune system of consciousness. A healthy immune system doesn't guarantee you'll never become ill, but it does reduce your susceptibility to illness and can improve your chances of a speedy recovery if you do become ill. The same is true psychologically. Those with strong self-esteem are much more resilient in the face of life's difficulties.

According to new evidence, healthy self-esteem is one of the best preventative measures for ensuring physical and mental health. In fact, strong self-esteem can help to boost your immune system, protect against heart disease, and accelerate healing. A growing body of evidence indicates that people with low self-esteem suffer more from chronic pain, headaches, respiratory infections, and digestive problems such as ulcers and irritable bowel syndrome.

Self-efficacy

Researchers in the field of mind–body medicine believe that one of the major components in healthy self-esteem is self-efficacy – your perception of your own abilities. A study by researchers at the University of California showed that self-efficacy actually causes a chemical change in the brain: it releases a chemical called catecholamine, which triggers a set of general physiological reactions that prepare your body for physical activity (fight or flight response). Some typical effects are increases in heart rate, blood pressure, and blood glucose levels. Illness can adversely affect self-efficacy by making us feel that we cannot do so many things we used to find easy.

'I used to feel as if I could do anything,' says Emma, a patient of mine who suffers from arthritis but who used to run her own PR company. 'It was easy for me to build myself up if I had a presentation or walked into a roomful of strangers. But now, I feel I am not as "worthy" as I once was. I look different, I can't do the things I once did, and worst of all, I feel different. I'm not the same person I was before my illness.'

Chronic illness and daily pain have a way of entering into life and draining the feelings of worthiness you once may have had. You may never have felt confident to begin with. Now having to park in a disabled bay or use a walking stick feels as if someone is knocking what self-esteem you had. What is it about pain that causes you perhaps to feel less of a person than you once did, and how can you regain the confidence you once had?

It is important to recognise that chronic pain conditions can contribute to low self-esteem. Years of pain that have obstructed meeting life's goals can have a disastrous effect on your self-esteem. Other factors that can arise as a direct result of chronic pain will also contribute to low-self esteem. They may include:

- loss of jobs or career opportunities

- unstable or failed relationships

- estrangement from unsupportive relationships with friends and family members

- inability to be financially self-supporting

- inability to take part in community activities

- cognitive difficulties.

When a chronic illness is involved, it may seem that you are unable to do anything worthwhile and you therefore label yourself as 'worthless'. Feeling worthless for long periods of time can lead to depression which can, in turn, become a kind of chronic low-level stress that makes the symptoms of ill-health worse. To help pinpoint possible contributors about your self-worth, ask yourself these questions:

- Is there anyone in your life who is feeding you negative or inappropriate messages about yourself?

- How do these messages make you feel?

- What are you going to do about it?

- What circumstances of your life have lowered your self-esteem and self-confidence?

- How valid were these circumstances in determining your sense of worth?

Boosting your self-esteem

As children, the reactions of our parents shaped our sense of self. Our minds and bodies were like tape recorders. We heard, saw and felt how the big people responded to us and their messages were recorded and absorbed. Some of the messages were positive and nurturing – 'That's a good girl.' 'You can do it.' 'Daddy loves you.' We learned to feel capable, adequate and worthwhile when we were loved, encouraged and accepted. On the other hand, if we received continual criticism and rejection – 'No. You're wrong,' 'You'll never get anywhere' – we learned to feel inadequate, uncertain and unworthy of a love-filled life.

All of these messages evolve into self-statements – thoughts, beliefs and attitudes – which may or may not be accurate. But once they are integrated, we accept them as true, regardless of the facts. It is believed that about 87 per cent of the things we say to ourselves, about ourselves, are negative. Putdowns and negative self-talk not only make us unhappy and discouraged, they become blocks to getting what we want. Accepting yourself and the fullness of life is a continuing process. Fortunately, there is a great deal you can do to make that process easier. Consider these ten suggestions:

- **List six to eight different aspects of your life** (e.g. work, health, body, relationships) and rank each area from 1 to 10, based on how satisfied you are with it. Notice if one or two areas bring down your 'average'. Focus on improving the lowest ones to improve your overall self-esteem.

- **Become aware of 'self-talk'.** This is the never-ending chatter in your head: thoughts, worries, plans, etc. Sometimes you'll notice a self-defeating dialogue – 'I'd like to meet him, but he won't like me.' Writing the thoughts on paper is helpful. Awareness of these beliefs is the first step to changing them.

- **Turn negative statements into positive ones.** 'I'm shy' becomes 'I'm warm and friendly.' 'I'm not attractive' becomes 'I'm learning to feel attractive.' When you feel anxious or self-conscious, take a deep breath and repeat several times, 'I like myself.' Don't worry if it doesn't feel comfortable at first. It takes time to reverse years of negative thinking. Stick with it. Thinking negative thoughts is a habit, and habits can be changed.

- **Avoid labelling,** calling yourself negative words and names: stupid, lazy, ugly. Delete self-defeating words from your vocabulary: should, never, can't, if only.

- **Identify your core beliefs.** These are central ideas underlying your feelings and actions. You'll begin to notice patterns where the same messages emerge in various areas of your life. One way to uncover core beliefs is to list one or two statements each parent told you. Examples are, 'I'm wrong.' 'I just can't do this.' 'People hurt me.' 'I don't deserve it.' 'I can't.' Awareness of these patterns helps you to pinpoint and solve problems when conflicts arise.

- **Choose a hobby or an interest.** Our self-worth changes when we do positive things, and enthusiasm is contagious. Friendships grow out of mutual interest.

- **Accept compliments gracefully.** Instead of disagreeing with the person, accept the positive feedback and merely say, 'Thank you.'

- **Develop an optimistic attitude.** Is your general attitude one of optimism or pessimism? Pay attention to the three Ps. When a setback occurs, do you experience it as *personal, permanent* and *pervasive*? An optimistic outlook can be developed with effort and increased awareness.

- **Create a support system of friends and family.** Your friends are your cheering section, people who encourage you, comfort and challenge you. When they say nice things, it's also another way to change a negative self-image.

- **Make your self-esteem unconditional.** Basing your self-worth on accomplishments is a vicious trap – always vacillating or delayed. 'I'll be happier with myself when . . .' Or 'I'll like myself better when . . .' A more compassionate attitude is to like yourself unconditionally, no matter what.

The best book on the subject of self-esteem is *Love is Letting Go of Fear* by Gerald G. Jampolsky (widely available).

Shirley's story

One of my patients who was to find optimism an invaluable tool in her healing process had suffered from severe head pains for almost 20 years. In that time, she and her husband hadn't even been able to go out for a meal together because of the distressing level of pain she was in. She was eventually diagnosed with systemic lupus, a chronic disorder of the immune system, and for two weeks she felt very low as she tried to think of a way to fight her illness.

> Suddenly a voice in my head asked me if I was going to let everything I'd learned over the previous two years fly out of the window. I was not! I gave myself a good talking to, took all the negative thoughts out of my head and replaced them with positive ones, and told myself this was a challenge that I was going to fight. Fortunately, I have now learned so much about relaxation, not to get stressed-out over silly things and not to needlessly worry. When I think of how I used to be, I cannot believe this is really me saying these things. I've changed so much and other people have noticed.

One of the first people to notice a change was her husband. Within a few sessions with me, together with her own efforts, her long-standing head pain had all but gone and they were able to enjoy a relaxed evening at a restaurant.

Chapter 4

Healing and Fear

Fear is an emotion indispensable for survival.
(Hannah Arendt, German philosopher)

A student once asked his old Yogi master how he maintained such peace of mind and physical well-being. The Yogi smiled and said, 'You only see the outside of my life. Inside my mind it is as if two powerful dogs are always fighting with each other.' The student asked what the dogs fought about, and the Yogi answered, 'One is always leading me to a better life – good health, strong energy, creativity, wonderful relationships, and continual joy and peace. The other is always leading me away from that wonderful place, to a horrible place that is its opposite. He has only one method, but it is a very powerful one. He leads me to *fear*. Once I am afraid, I cannot move. I am stuck and I can only spend my energy worrying and being upset, or trying to prevent what I am afraid of. This dog causes me much suffering.' 'Tell me, Master,' said the student, 'which dog most often wins?' The Yogi sighed, paused, then smiled and replied, 'Whichever one I feed.'

Fear and challenge

Fear is one of the most common human emotions and one we must all learn to deal with. For many people, it is often the simple thought of fear that prevents them from reaching out and taking actions to improve and better their lives. Every day I receive letters asking for my help, and often expressing feelings of fear: 'It scares me even to type this to you. I am desperate;' 'I keep thinking I'm going to die. My world has fallen apart;' 'I feel as if I've been hit with a cricket bat. I feel so wretched. I don't have any energy in me to do anything and feel I'm on a downward spiral;' 'I am beset by deep feelings of melancholy for no reason other than the diagnosis of my illness.'

These are fears and pains that I recognise only too well. I have seen and heard them in hundreds of patients newly diagnosed with a serious illness, all of whom have been suddenly presented with the greatest challenge of their life.

The first reaction with cancer, and many other serious illnesses, is a fear of losing your life. What treatment do I undertake? How do I make a choice? Is it effective? What else can I do to beat my illness? Much of my work in the initial stages with a patient is in helping them deal with fear, usually of the unknown. Most people have little or no knowledge of medical problems, or what is involved in treatment, and fear is not a good starting point for making important decisions. It can affect your judgement and lead to you make quick decisions without all the information you need to be properly aware of the implications.

Many of my patients regard their medical treatment with almost as much fear as they have for the illness itself. Most of their feelings seem to be associated with horror stories they have heard over the years. Although everyone responds differently to treatment, what may be arduous for one person may be easy for someone else. One of my first comments to a patient is often, 'It's never as bad as you think it's going to be.'

It is very important to try to replace fear with knowledge. I find that many of the things my patients fear about their diagnosis or treatment are simply not true. Your doctor should give you information about your illness and the anticipated benefits of whatever treatment you are being offered. Side-effects of treatment should also be made clear, although these are becoming less severe all the time.

The effects of fear

Most people go through several stages of fear when they are first diagnosed. I find that these stages, and the order in which they occur, are very similar in most people:

- You can't believe what you've just heard, and completely deny it.

- You get angry at the doctor who told you – and anyone else such as a nurse who gives you a test result.

- You appeal to a higher power and repeatedly ask, 'Why did this happen to me?' or 'What did I do to deserve this?

- You feel resigned, that there is nothing you can do to help yourself.

- You accept the truth, hard as it may be, and decide to fight with everything you've got.

A big part of fear when related to illness is all the uncertainty and the feeling that you have lost control of your life – being swept away on an uncharted journey that you don't want to take. Fear is the single most damaging, debilitating energy you have. It can interfere with your healing process and your well-being in every area of your life. You cannot thrive when you are controlled by fear because fear can stress your immune system, cloud your thinking, and create harmful biochemical responses. Fear feeds on attention. When you feed your fears with your attention, they become stronger. They gain power because you give it to them. What thoughts and beliefs in your mind are you feeding? Fears or faith? Worry or positive affirmations? Despair or trust in your own strength and power?

When you are in a state of fear your breathing becomes shallow and rapid, your mouth goes dry, you feel tightness around your neck, chest and abdomen, you feel clammy and nauseous, you tremble. Physical aches and pains, including headaches, can be triggered by fear.

The other significant effect is that you can't think straight. You can become irrational, your attention can be distorted, your mind wanders or switches off, you can't focus or concentrate, you may even panic. Being scared itself can scare you; it feeds on itself and spins out of control. You become isolated and find it hard to notice even if there is anyone around you

One of the first things to do is to distinguish between the *symptoms* of fear and the *healing* of fear. Tension, a dry mouth, nausea and pain are symptoms – indications that you have just experienced a fright or that old fears have been triggered or have resurfaced in some way or other. However, shaking and sweating are not symptoms. They are mechanisms for the release of fear, for draining away tension. Shaking and trembling, and sweating from either warm or cold skin, will relieve the nausea, relax the tense muscles and heal the fear in the mind. Laughter and crying can also help release the fear. The more you release during a fearful experience, the less you will need to do it later through nightmares, flashbacks, and unexpected shakes and sweats at awkward moments.

Fear and the mind–body connection

Although we have long known what effect fear has on our bodies, it has not been easy for medical researchers to identify in a laboratory setting exactly what effect fear has on the immune system, simply because of the difficulties of inducing fear in volunteers at a specific moment. However, psychologists at Amsterdam University have gained some insight by inducing social fear in subjects in an experimental setting. Social fear was induced in volunteers by asking them to prepare to give a speech in front of an audience – a remarkably common fear. Other volunteers formed a control group. They followed exactly the same procedure, but instead of being asked to speak in public, they were given an undemanding task of the same duration. Those who had to actually give a speech were closely monitored and found to have enhanced cardiovascular activity, increased plasma hormone levels, and changes in NK cell and T-helper/inducer cell numbers. If giving a short talk in public can cause sufficient fear to influence your immune system, you can imagine what a more deeply held fear sustained over a long period of time could do.

Henry Beecher, the doctor who first used the word 'placebo', observed soldiers during World War II who were suffering from wounds which would normally require strong medication if experienced by civilians. However, only a quarter of those soldiers needed morphine for their pain. Tissue damage was similar and yet the wounded soldiers' need for medication was significantly lower. Something had replaced the effect of the drug.

Beecher's insight was that the *meaning* of the pain for a soldier was very different from that experienced by a person severely injured in a car accident. For the soldier the wound was a way of returning home, a way to get out of the front line of war. For a car crash victim with similar injuries, the accident would mean loss of work, greater medical expenses, the loss of free time at home, and more. A consideration of the experiences of different soldiers is also interesting. Those who were *less* badly injured experienced *more* pain and needed more pain-controlling drugs. These soldiers knew that the less serious wounds meant that they would be patched up and sent back to fight. They felt the pain more and needed more pain medication.

Another study, published by Israeli researchers in 2004, showed that Israeli women with chronic fears of terror attacks had higher levels of a blood protein that can lead to heart disease. It has been the first study to demonstrate, in a large group of apparently healthy people, that the psychological reaction of chronic fear of terror has a negative impact on health.

Fight or flight

If you feel threatened, your sense of fear will accelerate your metabolism in anticipation of an imminent need to defend yourself or flee. The acute stress response, popularly known as 'fight or flight', was first described by the American physiologist Walter Cannon in the 1920s. Cannon observed that animals, including humans, react to threats with a hormonal discharge of the nervous system. There is an outpouring of vessel-constricting, heart-thumping hormones. Your heart speeds up and pumps harder, your nerves fire more quickly, your skin cools and gets goose bumps, your eyes dilate to see better and your brain receives a message that it is time to act.

Accepting ourselves as animals is crucial to understanding how fear is designed to work. The fear centre of the human brain, the amygdale, is identical to the fear centres of other animal brains. An almond-shaped brain structure that interprets emotion, it has been described as the hub in the brain's wheel of fear. When it is stimulated, there is an outpouring of stress hormones, causing a state of hyper-vigilance. The amygdale processes the primitive emotions of fear, hate, love, bravery and anger – all neighbours in the deep limbic brain that we derive from lower animals. When the amygdale malfunctions, a mood disorder, or state of uncontrollable apprehension, results.

The amygdale senses via the thalamus (the brain's receiver), thinks through the cortex (the brain's seat of reasoning) and remembers via the hippocampus (the brain's filing cabinet). Once a person has learned to fear something, he may always feel fear associated with that experience. But, unlike mice, we humans can fear events we have only read or heard about, so we worry about disasters we may never experience. If we are unable to respond for lack of an appropriate target, the fear accumulates. Ironically, at a time in history when true scourges are quite rare, the population is largely controlled by fear – for example about the spread of bird flu. Rather than enjoy the safety that our scientific and technological advances have given us, we feel uncertain.

It used to be that a person could die from a scratch. Now we take effective antibiotics at the first sign of trouble. We have drinkable water and breathable air, and our rubbish is quickly removed. We live temperature-controlled, largely disease-controlled lives. Yet we worry more than ever before. The natural dangers are no longer there, but the response mechanisms are turned on much of the time. We implode, turning our adaptive fear mechanism into a maladaptive panic response. The irony is, by worrying so much about our health we jeopardise our well-being. The mass media tend to magnify the latest health concern and broadcast it to millions of people at once. This provokes fear way out of proportion to the actual risks.

Back in the 1930s an English physician, Dr Grantley Dick-Read, realised that the more fearful a woman was, the more tense her body and the more pain she felt during childbirth. Her state of fear meant that blood was being diverted away from internal organs and the uterus was trying to work with less oxygen. The chemicals released during a state of fear can also work to stop labour from occurring. Although it may sound strange, it is a throwback to a wild animal giving birth in a forest. If the animal senses danger, the 'fight or flight' response can stop labour to allow the animal to retreat to a safe place. Once the danger is gone, labour resumes, the offspring is delivered and both mother and her baby are safe.

On a day-to-day basis, if your body is under stress it produces hormones such as adrenalin and cortisol. Too much of either of these hormones can be harmful.

Fear and anxiety

The American psychologist Mary Meagher, who has conducted pain research for almost 20 years, says two emotional states – fear and anxiety – have profoundly different effects on your ability to feel pain. Fear actually reduces pain, whereas anxiety has a sensitising or enhancing effect. Fear is an immediate alarm reaction to a present threat, characterised by a desire to escape and accompanied by specific physiological changes. Anxiety is a future-orientated emotion characterised by anticipation of potential threats. Fear mobilises you to take action, but anxiety leads you to scan your environment and body, resulting in increased sensory input. Confronted with a life-threatening situation, which would elicit fear, your body temporarily shuts off the pain response because feeling pain might get in the way of your survival.

This is exactly what happened to the nineteenth-century explorer David Livingstone, who was attacked by a lion in southern Africa. He described his reaction to being grabbed by the shoulder and mauled. 'The shock produced a stupor similar to that felt by a mouse after the first shake of the cat. It caused a sort of dreaminess in which there was no pain, though I was quite conscious of what was happening. It was like patients partially under the influence of chloroform describe, who see all the operation, but feel not the knife.' When the lion let go for a moment, Livingstone managed to escape.

Most of us are no longer fighting or running for our lives in the wild, but fear is far from an outdated instinct. It serves the same purpose today as it did when Livingstone was mauled by the lion, or our ancestors threatened by a sabre-toothed tiger. We are now carrying a wallet and walking through a city street. The decision not to take that shortcut through an empty alleyway at midnight is based on a rational fear that promotes survival. Only the stimuli have changed – in that situation, we are in as much danger today as we were hundreds of years ago, and our fear serves to protect us as it did then. Most of us have never been anywhere near bubonic plague, yet our heart will jump a beat at the sight of a rat.

Fear and panic

Fear can also be contagious – we have all heard of how 'panic spreads'. In 1998, a teacher at a school in Tennessee noticed a petrol-like smell in her classroom and complained of a headache, nausea, shortness of breath and dizziness. Several students in her class soon reported similar problems and school officials ended up evacuating the entire building amid the noise of firefighters, police and ambulances. A local hospital admitted 80 students and 19 staff members; 38 were kept in overnight. When the school eventually reopened five days later, the hospital treated another 71 individuals who developed symptoms that were attributed to toxic gas exposure. While people at the school suffered from genuine physical ailments, an extensive investigation conducted by several government agencies uncovered no medical or environmental explanation, a research team reported in the *New England Journal of Medicine*. Instead, the outbreak of illness stemmed from fear about possible exposure to poison. These feelings and related physical symptoms spread contagiously in a closely congregated group, said the researchers. 'Even if the students responded to contagious fear, they experienced authentic pain and suffering,' commented Dr

Simon Wessely of Guy's, King's and St Thomas' School of Medicine in London.

Fear as an early warning system

For humans, as Mary Meagher discovered, there are other factors involved in fear that go beyond instinct. We sometimes have the unfortunate gift of *anticipation*, and we anticipate terrible things that *might* happen – things we have heard about, read about, or seen on TV. Most of us have never experienced a plane crash, but that doesn't stop us from sitting on a plane with white-knuckle grips on the armrests. Anticipating a fearful stimulus can provoke the same response as actually experiencing it.

Many people experience fear not because they are ill or about to undergo surgery, but because they are unable to distinguish health warnings that are grounded in impending danger from those that are not. Fear is an expectation of alarm or dànger and works best as a warning system, a response to dangers that directly threaten those who are afraid. However, we tend to pour our fears into dangers that, however real, pose a relatively low risk for any individual – like terrorism, mad cow disease, and now bird flu. So where do our fears originate?

Studies have shown that, perhaps surprisingly, we are born with only two fears: the fear of falling and the fear of loud noises. The rest of our fears are learned. When you look at fear from that perspective, it makes one wonder why we often surrender ourselves to fear so easily. Unremitting fear has the same effect on your body as always driving your car at 100 miles per hour. For a person who is always on the alert, who suffers from a too easily triggered and sustained fight-or-flight response, the result is a burned-out body. Many illnesses are more likely to occur as a result, including heart disease, cancer, stroke and depression. What we have to fear most are not the exotic diseases that scare us but the ordinary killers such as heart attacks that develop as a result of our endless worries and fears.

Fear and surgery

Every year many of my patients are told that they need surgery, and an unsettling image pops into their mind. Typically, they see themselves alone and vulnerable, wearing a flimsy hospital gown, with any sense of control given over to a team of relative strangers. That sense of anxiety and fear flooded over Joan when she learned that she needed extensive surgery to remove a malignant brain tumour. 'I was really afraid,' she later told me. 'The reality is, it was the closest I was ever going to come to dying. I really needed some way to relax in order to take the fear away.'

Having surgery is one of life's most difficult experiences. It is a time of ultimate vulnerability and loss of control, and it brings us face to face with our mortality. There is also fear of pain, the unknown, disability, disfigurement, loss and embarrassment, all the while in the context of separation from family. This is a huge psychological burden that patients must face, in addition to the difficulties of the medical problem. Traditionally, hospitals have addressed pre-operative issues merely with a consent form that lists the risks, or have simply provided handout sheets to give practical information about what will be happening to your body. You must also prepare yourself emotionally.

Experts in mind–body medicine contend that getting prepared for surgery doesn't have to be so frightening. They endorse a range of mind–body techniques that will help you cope, and even improve the outcome – if you are open to the possibilities. The key is to learn how you can participate in your own healing, and how your emotions and attitudes can enhance your body's healing process. Studies show that the transformation from passive patient to active healing participant can generate dramatic results. By coping with fear directly, research indicates, it is possible to feel peaceful before and *during* surgery and recovery is often quicker. Blood loss is reduced, less pain is perceived, and fewer painkillers are needed. Moreover, your immune system seems to respond better.

These benefits contrast starkly with the disadvantages of approaching surgery swamped with worries. When this happens, increased stress hormones can precipitate such undesirable reactions as heightened pain perception, complications during and after surgery, excessive bleeding, and even slow-to-heal wounds. Anxiety and fear, especially anxiety that has built up over days or weeks prior to surgery, can:

- lead to increased cortisol levels, which interfere with immune function, putting you at greater risk of infection and decreased wound healing. On the day of surgery, cortisol levels can rise up to *ten-fold* above the average in the most fearful or frightened patients

- lead to increased smoking and alcohol use at a time when you need to cut down on both. Alcohol use decreases immune function, delays wound healing and interferes with anaesthesia; smokers have decreased blood flow to organs, including the skin, impaired wound healing, and increased post-operative infections

- lead to increased output of catecholamine, which can increase the risk of high blood pressure and irregular heartbeat

- cause the anaesthetist to give you more medication, which will take longer to leave your system and lead to increased side-effects of nausea, headache, etc.

- inhibit higher cortical brain function, leaving you unable to think clearly to make important decisions for your health

- lead to increased feelings of pain. Many studies have demonstrated a direct correlation between anxiety and the intensity of pain felt

For over 20 years, studies have shown that surgical patients who have been prepared so that they are calmer have less pain, heal more quickly, have fewer complications and leave hospital earlier. Since the healing process is a cascade of events, final wound healing is very dependent on the initial repair process, which can be sabotaged by early problems. Two recent studies show the dramatic benefits of relaxation for surgery, to decrease pain and anxiety and improve healing.

In the first, published in 1997 in *Diseases of the Colon and Rectum*, 130 patients at the Cleveland Clinic Foundation who listened to a relaxation and guided imagery tape before having major bowel surgery had a significantly better experience than those who did not. They had less pain, less anxiety, used less medication and had quicker recovery of bowel function – 58 hours, as opposed to 92 hours. The second study, published in the *Western Journal of Medicine*, involved sedated invasive surgery, where patients were awake but given intravenous pain medication. Three groups were used – a control group, a group with someone sitting next to the patient giving them attention, and a group with someone sitting next to the patient but suggesting relaxation imagery. All groups could have as much pain medication as they wanted. The relaxation group experienced significantly less pain and anxiety, used less medication, spent less time in the operating theatre, and had very significantly fewer complications. It was calculated that this created an estimated saving of over $1200!

So how can you prepare yourself for surgery, or other medical treatment, using mind–body techniques? You can use whatever method you are already familiar with, such as meditation or yoga. Many of my patients use my relaxation and self-healing recordings. The point is not to be utterly relaxed, but more in 'calm confidence' or 'relaxed readiness' mode. One researcher, Dr Henry Bennett, has suggested that you 'think of yourself as an athlete in training for a major event, rather than as a passive body being handed over to the surgical team'. If you don't want to listen to someone's voice on a relaxation tape, I would recommend you listen to music via headphones. Many studies have shown that people can hear under anaesthesia.

I once watched a surgeon carrying out an operation and was surprised to discover that, rather than talking about a game of golf – an irreverent but popular image of the surgeon in an operating theatre – he was talking to the unconscious and anaesthetised patient, making suggestions to reduce blood flow and accelerate healing. One of the surgical team told me about a report showing that patients undergoing abdominal hysterectomy used 23 per cent less pain medication (compared to a control group) if positive 'healing statements' were made by the operating team during the procedure.

Many surgeons believe that in the operating theatre you may subconsciously hear something upsetting, or misinterpret what is said. Anaesthetic drugs sometimes make sounds seem very loud. Listening to music blocks out the confusion of the operating theatre and helps you maintain a peaceful state. In addition, nurses note that patients who listen to music in the recovery room are less agitated and need less pain medication. If you choose to use music, pick something calming, with a rate of 70 beats per minute or less. Your heart rate has a tendency to mimic the rate of the music you are listening to, and you want to maintain calm heart rate and blood pressure.

Ways to manage fear with your medical team

- As you start to gather information to make decisions about surgery or other treatment, get to know who the people in your medical team are and try to meet them all in person. Try to turn faceless doctors into known resources. You'll find out who is the best communicator, who can answer which questions, and who is available to help you when you need it most.

• Try to find a doctor who communicates with you in a way that is comfortable for you, who invites your questions and takes your concerns seriously, who gives you as much or as little information as you feel comfortable with.

• Find out what to expect from tests, treatments and procedures. Minimise surprises.

• If possible, try to schedule important tests early in the week, so you don't have to wait over a long weekend, when laboratory work may slow down or doctors aren't communicating with each other.

• When you know you're going to have a challenging week (for example a biopsy, chemotherapy or radiotherapy), don't plan to do things that may be stressful for you. Use your support systems (family or friends) – anything that helps you to get through it.

• If well-meaning people try to tell you horror stories about what other people have been through, stop them straight away and say: 'I only listen to stories with happy endings!'

• If you get to a point where difficult emotions are getting in the way of your functioning or taking care of yourself, don't be ashamed to talk to your doctor about the role of medication that might ease your anxiety, depression or sleeping problems. As a healer, I always tell my patients, 'There's a time and a place for everything.'

- Work on ways to feel more positive about your life. Search for productive, life-enhancing experiences; spend time with positive people who affirm who you are and how you've chosen to deal with your illness.

Releasing fear

A few simple thought exercises can help you identify, target, and overcome any fears more effectively:

- **Identify your fear.** Overcoming fear starts here. When you name it, you can release it. Are you fearful of losing your job? Death? Being harmed in some way? Being abandoned? Failure? The unknown? Identifying your fear is the first step in loosening its grip on you and your reality.

- **Get it out.** Listing your fears on paper is a powerful way to get them out of your mind and out of your way. You may find that all you have to do to dissipate a fear is to write it down and share it. Other fears need more exploration, which you may need to do with a professional therapist.

- **Talk about it.** Sharing your fear out loud can make it seem much less daunting.

- **Learn about the thing you fear.** Uncertainty is a huge component of fear. Developing an understanding of what you're afraid of goes a long way towards erasing that fear.

- **Find someone who is not fearful.** If there is something you are afraid of, find someone who is not afraid of that thing and spend time with that person. Take them with you when you try to conquer your fear — it will be much easier.

- **Train.** If there is something you are afraid to try because it seems scary or difficult, start small and work in steps. Slowly building familiarity with a frightening subject makes it more manageable.

- **Play mind games with yourself.** If you are afraid of speaking in front of people, it is probably because you think the audience is going to judge you. Try imagining the audience members naked – being the only clothed person in the room puts *you* in the position of judgement.

- **Stop looking at the grand scheme.** Think only about each successive step. If you are afraid of heights, don't think about being on the fortieth floor of a building. Just think about getting your foot in the lobby.

You will also find the following meditation exercise will help you to uncover memories that can counteract the fear of what *might* happen tomorrow, fear that prevents you from making changes in your life today or that could have a positive impact on the future.

Uncovering positive memories

You can either read the following piece as you would an article, or you can ask a friend to read it for you. Or, you can read it several times to yourself, pausing when it comes to breaks identified by a three-point ellipsis (...) in order to have time to experience that section in whatever way feels comfortable to you. This will probably take you about 20 minutes. I have also recorded it (see Resources).

Begin by becoming as comfortable as possible ... As you allow your body to feel fully supported, notice the quieting sensation of your hands at rest and let your muscles relax all the way down to your toes . . . As you continue to relax more . . . and more . . . allow your mind to become quiet and still . . . Soon you find yourself in a pleasantly relaxed frame of mind. Now, I invite you to follow this exercise in whatever way feels right for you.

The first part of this exercise is intended to help you remember some of the many times you have controlled your life, at least to a large degree. I will shortly ask you to recall various times when you responded with confidence and skill to challenges sent your way. Later in the exercise you will create a very special image that you can use whenever fear threatens to overpower you. As you follow the first part of this exercise, accept your memories as gifts from your subconscious, gifts it offers you as a way out of fear.

And now, because knowledge can diminish the power of fear, recall a time when you solved a difficult problem by learning something new . . . As you remember this, experience how it feels to have the ability to learn and grow . . . Be aware that fear would have you believe that you have to face life all by yourself. But you are not alone. Instead of holding fear inside, where it can grow and take control, when you share it with others you diminish fear's power over your life. And so, recall a time when, because you expressed your feelings and your needs clearly, you were supported by others . . . And as you remember, feel love and gratitude flowing through your body because you have caring people in your life.

Turn your attention now to something else that fear would have you forget. You see, concern about the future comes in large part from worrying that you might make mistakes. And you might. But you can challenge this concern by validating yourself as a person who not only has many natural talents in solving problems but who also has an ability to learn from mistakes. Recall now a time when you made a mistake, were able to forgive yourself and learned from it.

And notice now that fear wants you to focus on the separate details of life, seeing one thing as good and another as bad, with particular emphasis on the bad. Of course, we all have a tendency to see one part of our life as acceptable and another as unacceptable. But, like everyone else, you have also had experiences that transcended that sense of separateness, times when you experienced the ordinary, individual details of life as a whole. You may have felt this connection with the essence of life when you held a newborn child or when you stood overlooking an ocean, wondering how many millions of other people had looked at that same ocean for countless centuries. And so, recall now a time when you connected with this sense of oneness.

Finally, turn your attention to one of the most powerful things you can do to keep fear from bringing the future into the present – you can choose to accept the future only when it actually arrives. Furthermore, you banish fear by choosing to celebrate the pleasures that life offers in each moment, for fear is a very serious emotion, with no sense of pleasure and certainly no sense of humour. It doesn't want you to smile at the little bird scurrying along the beach at the water's edge or share a silly story with an old friend. Why? Because you cannot be overwhelmed by fears of the future if you are fully focused on the present. And so, bring your attention now to this present moment . . . this time has never been before and will never be again . . . As you focus on this moment, allow a feeling of peace and serenity to gently flow throughout your body . . .

As you continue to feel centred and calm, we come to the last part of this exercise – creating an image that can reduce the power that fear wants to have over you. Begin by noticing that in the entire landscape of your life, there is some healthy concern about what might happen. But there is also much, much more. And so, with a deep appreciation for your ability to respond positively to all of life, allow an image of strength and confidence to bubble up from deep within. This may appear as an object you actually experience with your senses or you may just get a general feeling of what it could be. However this image appears, experience it as fully and powerfully as you can . . .

As you hold this image in your mind, allow yourself to be filled with confidence and peace. Feel how wonderful it is to know that while you may not have control over everything that happens to you, you have the power to choose how to live. In that choosing, you take away from fear its ability to control your sense of well-being. And so, when you first become afraid of any of the many things that fear would have you worry about, recall the image you have created and hold it in your heart. If, once in a while, you find yourself lost in fear or emotionally stuck, you can repeat this exercise. You may then discover that you can create an even more powerful image that can help you realise fear need not be your master. When you have an image that brings you peace and comfort, you may want to use it when other strong emotions try to focus all your attention on their agenda for your life.

And now, turn your attention back to the room you are in, bringing with you one particular thing about fear that would be good for you to remember . . . and then feel your body supported by the chair . . . take a deep energising breath. Stretch your arms and legs and return to full awareness, realising that you will always be aware of problems that may come your way from time to time. You do not need to be a prisoner to fear.

Most of my patients, when I first meet them, are in some state of fear. The degree of fear they are experiencing often correlates with their diagnosis or prognosis. Usually fear is doing as much, if not more, damage as the illness itself. Quite often, on our first meeting, I hear them use the word 'dread'. I've always felt that dread is negative expectancy. Fear combined with dread can be a lethal combination – sometimes literally.

Most frightened people will usually anticipate the worst. Removing or understanding your fear is rather like taking your foot off the brake pedal while driving your car. It allows natural optimism and positive attitudes to play a greater role in your life. In our everyday life we tend to base our actions on the *probability* of events occurring with the knowledge that there is a remote *possibility* of negative situations arising. You can take these negative possibilities into account, but don't let them dictate your life. Walking down the street you are aware that there is a very remote possibility of a tile falling off a roof – but you don't stay indoors or wear a crash helmet when going out! The probability is that all will be well so you follow that belief. If you have underlying fear it will often push negative possibilities into the probability category – and you will then act as if it is a probability.

Fear is a paramount response when dealing with illness – on all sides – but it can be overcome by a simple four-point approach:

1. Be *aware* that fear exists.

2. *Express* that fear and seek support from others.

3. Seek any information that will enable you to gain *understanding* and *control* over it.

4. Having dealt with your feelings, allow yourself to go ahead and *enjoy* your life, experiences and activities.

Chapter 5
Healing and Anger

Holding onto anger is like grasping a hot coal with the intent of throwing it at someone else. You are the only one who gets burnt.
(Buddha)

The eighteenth-century physician John Hunter was a pioneer in the field of surgery and served as surgeon to King George III. He suffered from angina and, discovering that his attacks were often brought on by anger, he lamented, 'My life is at the mercy of any scoundrel who chooses to annoy me.' His words proved prophetic. In 1793, at a meeting of the board of St George's Hospital in London, Hunter got into a heated argument with other board members, walked out, and dropped dead in the next room. His case was the first to be described in both its pre- and post-mortem phases. His biographer, playing down the doctor's easily aroused anger, described his 'temper' as 'very warm and impatient, readily provoked, and when irritated not easily soothed'.

Two hundred years later, the singer Billy Joel wrote a song called 'Angry Young Man' which tells the story of a young man who has never been able to learn from his mistakes. He cannot understand why his heart always breaks, and is therefore destined to go to the grave as 'an angry old man'. A recent study at the Johns Hopkins

School of Medicine suggests that Billy Joel was close to the truth when he wrote that song. The study, which tracked 1,337 male medical students for three years following medical school, found that students who became angry quickly under stress were three times more likely to develop premature heart disease and five times more likely to have an early heart attack. Angry young men, it appears, turn into angry old men with heart problems.

So why does this happen? Is there a correlation between anger and heart disease or other illnesses? From hundreds of medical studies over the past twenty years, it is now known that frequent or chronic anger can have serious consequences for your health.

Anger and health

- People most prone to anger are almost three times more likely to have a heart attack than those who become angry less easily, according to a recent study of 12,986 participants in *Circulation*.

- Medical students who became angry quickly when under stress were three times more likely to develop premature heart disease and five times more likely to have an early heart attack than their calmer colleagues, researchers reported in the *Archives of Internal Medicine* in 2002. Hot tempers predicted heart disease even before traditional risk factors such as diabetes and high blood pressure. Among several hundred medical students at the University of North Carolina who were rated for anger and hostility levels while in their early twenties, those with the greatest chronic anger were seven times more likely than their peers to be dead 25 years later.

- Researchers at Stanford University found they could induce perceptible constrictions in the coronary arteries of cardiac

patients merely by asking them to recall a recent event that
had made them angry.

• An Israeli study suggests a link between experiencing an angry
moment and an immediate risk of stroke. Neurologist Silvia
Koton interviewed 200 people hospitalised with strokes and
asked the patients if they had experienced anger or negative
emotions two hours before the 'event'. Some 30 per cent of
the patients reported anger, suggesting that exposure to such
triggers could increase the risk of stroke by as much as 14-fold
within two hours.

• Professor Madhulika Gupta of the Western University of
Ontario demonstrated in a 1997 report that repressed anger
may trigger both the onset and individual 'flare-ups' of
psoriasis. Expression of anger was shown to be the most
important correlate of early-onset, as compared with late-
onset, psoriasis. (The condition can start at any point in life,
but researchers labelled those who experienced the disease
before the age of 40 as 'early-onset' cases.) Patients with early-
onset psoriasis were found to have much more repressed anger.
Those with psoriasis who have difficulty expressing their anger
tend to experience more flare-ups of the disease as well as
being less responsive to treatments.

• Men who live their life in a permanent state of anger or
hostility face a high risk of developing heart disease. New
research conducted in Canada suggests that women whose life
consists of simmering anger do not face the same risk.
However, anger and stress in women may be linked to other
diseases. A study reported in the journal *Heart* found a
connection with diabetes.

• A recent report published in the *British Journal of Dermatology* claimed a link between anger and acne. 'Care of acne patients should include attention to anger and other chronic emotional states, as well as to clinical severity', said the authors.

- American researchers reported in the *Journal of Advancement in Medicine* a connection between anger and increased risk of illness. They measured the production of S-Iga (salivary immunoglobulin A), heart rate and mood in response to experiences of two different emotions. S-Iga is the body's first line of defence against viruses and bacteria in the lungs, digestive and urinary tracts. When the subjects simply replayed an argument in their minds for five minutes, their immune systems were suppressed for up to six hours. When the subjects thought of sincerity and care, their immune systems were significantly boosted. This finding has further implications. High levels of S-Iga seem to correlate positively with the spread of breast cancer, suggesting that anger suppression may be related to the spread of cancer.

- A study presented at the annual International AIDS Conference found that anger in sexually active gay and bisexual men who were HIV positive was associated with the presence of fewer helper T-cells (white blood cells that help to coordinate the various activities of your immune system) – and more killer T-cells (cells that inhibit or suppress immune responses).

- Dr George Solomon, Professor Emeritus of psychiatry and behavioural sciences at the University of California, has found that people who did nothing when provoked into anger underwent a decrease in immune system defensive cells, while those subjects who asserted themselves showed no change in blood chemistry. 'People who have repressive styles tend to be more prone to illness, particularly (immune system related) diseases such as rheumatoid arthritis, infections, and some cancers. The concept isn't of expressed anger, but unexpressed anger. If one doesn't let it out, it could have adverse consequences', he says.

The physiology of anger

These are some of the physiological effects triggered when you are angry:

- Extra adrenalin is secreted and the body speeds up, preparing to defend itself.

- Extra cholesterol and catecholamines are released into the blood stream. Research has shown that these chemicals accelerate the development of fatty deposits in the heart and carotid arteries.

- The heart beats more quickly and blood pressure rises.

- Breathing becomes faster.

- The sympathetic nervous system diverts blood from the liver, intestines and stomach to the heart, central nervous system and muscles.

- Cortisol is increased, depressing the immune system.

- Men have an increased supply of testosterone.

This state of heightened arousal puts great strain on your body. It is useful as a short-term emergency reaction, but not as a long-term personality trait or a lifestyle characteristic. There are, moreover, some physical conditions that will lower the threshold for triggering anger. They include:

- over-tiredness

- hunger

- sexual frustration

- hormonal changes due to puberty, PMT, the menopause, and childbirth

- physical craving for addictive substances such as alcohol, nicotine, caffeine or other drugs

- intoxication

- physical illness

- living with acute or chronic pain

- dementia

Although some people may blame their inability to manage their anger on the above factors, it should be noted that many people with these conditions still succeed in controlling their anger. Anyone who is capable of mental concentration and motivated to learn can be taught to manage angry and aggressive feelings. Out of control, you are at the mercy of your anger. You need a new kind of relationship with your emotions: one where you run them, instead of them running you. Anger is an emotional or behavioural reaction of displeasure to an unmet expectation, demand or belief and it has three components: thinking, feeling and acting.

The psychology of anger

Psychologically, anger has two aspects: thinking and feeling. The thinking part is negative thoughts and beliefs about others. When you are angry, you may think: 'I'll have to ask her three times and then get angry before she'll tidy her room,' 'You can't trust him! He's always out to get what he can for himself!' or 'People like that don't deserve any protection.' If you think this way, your judgements may increase your feelings of threat and actions of defensiveness.

The feeling part of anger includes disappointment, annoyance, irritation, resentment, frustration, contempt and rage. You may turn your thoughts and feelings into action. When people are angry, they may say a variety of things, point their finger or shake their fist, and say, 'You idiot! Get your car out of my way!' or 'What did you call me? We'll see about that!'

Anger is one of the most misunderstood and overused of human emotions. We all have angry feelings sometimes. Anger is a normal adaptive emotion and not in itself a problem; it is the behavioural response to anger that determines whether or not it is problematic. In some situations anger empowers us to challenge injustice or to make necessary changes in our lives. However, at other times anger becomes aggression. Anger with aggression is usually a response to perceived threat, unfairness or injustice. Extreme actions that express anger include assault and violence, and we seem to be living in an increasingly angry society. Anger turned inwards may result in a lack of appropriate assertiveness, stress or depression.

Anger and aggression originally evolved to help our ancestors cope with life-threatening events. In our modern world, very few of us experience those sorts of physical threat. In today's society we can perhaps substitute 'life-threatening' with 'identity-threatening' – some of the things that make people feel angry and stimulate aggressive thoughts are:

- perceived disrespectful treatment of thoughts, beliefs, feelings and needs

- perceived threat to the continuation or success of something to which we are strongly committed, for example our partner, job, lifestyle, etc.

- perceived unfairness

- perceived provocation or suspicion and hostility. 'They' did that on purpose, just to 'wind me up'. The best form of defence is to attack before they do.

Anger is one of the biggest obstacles to personal success, relationships, health, even your career. If you fail to control your anger, you can suffer several blows simultaneously:

- Anger impedes your ability to be happy, because anger and happiness are incompatible.

- Anger sends marriages and other family relationships off course.

- Anger reduces social skills, compromising other relationships.

- Anger leads to increased stress, which is ironic since stress often increases anger.

- When angry, you are more likely to make mistakes because anger makes it harder for you to process information.

For some people anger is not a problem: they get angry, sort it out quickly and then return to equilibrium. Anger becomes problematic when it is too easily triggered or prolonged. It then impacts on concentration, mood, relationships, work and social life – and health. Anger reactions have been likened to a train running out of control and about to derail. While a little anger can motivate us to take action in positive ways, a lot of anger will make us 'red with rage'. Anger that is out of control will drive away those whom we love the most and endanger our normal daily existence.

Feeling – Anger In and Anger Out

What is your definition of anger? Do you know what usually makes you angry? Can you identify who usually makes you angry? Are you aware of the 'triggers' that are likely to arouse your anger? How do you usually express your anger? Psychologists now know that there are two types of anger. 'Anger In' is anger directed inwardly towards oneself, manifested by depression or suppressed hostility. 'Anger Out' is anger directed outwardly towards other people or things.

Anger refers to an emotional state consisting of feelings that vary in intensity from mild irritation or annoyance to intense fury and rage. Hostility refers to an emotional state involving angry feelings, and resulting in a complex set of attitudes that motivate aggressive behaviour directed at people or things. Aggression refers to a set of behaviour traits directed at destroying objects and injuring or 'punishing' people.

If you are angry, you need to first face the anger for what it is and not avoid it. You will need to identify the feelings at the root of your anger. Some angry people refuse to get help with their anger because anger works for them. They use it as intimidation to control family members and to get what they want. These people are known as 'Anger Outers', blasting their anger in all directions. They have learned that intimidation works so they see no reason to do anything to change their behaviour. They feel better after their anger release and forget what happened quickly. In their mind, the problem is over for them, and they cannot understand that others remain traumatised or hurt by their actions. They do not believe that they have a problem; it is OK to get their anger out so they can feel better.

Some people, stuck in their destructive anger pattern, don't realise that there are other options. They decide that this is how they are and they can't change. Their closed mind makes any new information coming in a threat. They usually don't believe in getting professional help, as they do not feel comfortable discussing their emotions or admitting they might be at fault.

People who express anger outwardly usually link up with 'Anger Inners'. Those who turn their anger inward suppress their anger, which results in anxiety, poor self-esteem, bitterness and depression. Anger Inners can become martyrs, victims who hold their pent-up anger until it builds up in resentment and explodes. After years of holding it in, the stress of living with repressed anger can add to physical illness.

When I was younger, I used to have a very short fuse before erupting into anger, even though I knew a lot about relaxation, meditation, and putting myself into a healing space. One day, for reasons that I have long since forgotten, I became really angry over something and began shouting at my then wife, although what I was angry about was nothing to do with her or anything she had said or done. She looked at me and told me how pathetic I was for over-reacting so angrily to such a trivial occurrence. I realised that she was right and decided to do something about it.

I knew that when I was getting angry, I could actually feel it mounting inside me like a hot liquid being pushed up the sides of a container – eventually spilling out and scalding anyone who came too close. (Years later, one of my patients described her anger as 'a bubbling in my body like a mob of prisoners', another variation on the theme.)

I would use an old, some may say over-simplistic method of dealing with anger at this point: I would literally hold my breath and count – very slowly – backwards from 10 to 1. For me, the result was quite a revelation. I realised that anger was frequently masking quite a different emotion or feeling. Although I thought I was angry, I wasn't – I was actually insecure, fearful, resentful, or any one of a myriad other emotions. I found that I was often able to identify jealousy, pride, guilt, resentment, fear, embarrassment or depression in my anger. Once I had identified them, I needed to confront the issues that stimulated the anger.

Managing your anger

You can gain a quick insight into your anger levels with the following check list:

Check your anger levels

Look at these statements and note down how many apply to you:

- *People tell you that you need to calm down.*

- *You feel tense much of the time.*

- *At work, you find yourself not saying what is on your mind.*

- *When you are upset, you try to block the world out by watching TV, reading a book or magazine, or going to sleep.*

- *You are drinking almost daily to help you calm down.*

- *You have trouble getting to sleep.*

- *You feel misunderstood or not listened to much of the time.*

- *People ask you not to shout and swear so much.*

- *Your loved ones keep saying that you are hurting them.*

- *Friends don't seek you out as much.*

If you agreed with between 0 and 2 of these statements, your anger is manageable. Between 3 and 5 suggests that you need to learn more about what stresses you and about relaxation. A score of 6 or more suggests that you have an anger problem and you could benefit by learning about anger management.

There are many popular ways to manage anger: count to ten, take three deep breaths, walk away from the situation, have a break. How many times, when were you angry, did your anger give you the energy and the motivation to redirect your actions constructively? As well as holding your breath and counting backwards if your anger is aroused, you might well find that these steps, known as STAR, are helpful:

- **Stop**. Notice when you are starting to feel angry and look for the tell-tale signs. Is your voice rising, neck tightening, face getting hot, hand shaking, jaw tightening or clenching, and breath shortening? Do you want to run away? If so, relax yourself using deep, natural breathing and muscle relaxation. Take deep breaths and silently repeat the word 'relax' until you are able to calm down. Do not say anything until you are calm. Avoid words or actions in the heat of the moment.

- **Think.** Try to imagine the consequences if you lose control. Most of us don't want to hurt our children, spouse, colleagues or others, either physically or emotionally. If you try to picture the consequences both for you and for the person with whom you are angry, it can help you engage your brain before you engage your tongue or fist.

- **Ask.** Ask yourself what you are really angry about. Is it a situation, an event, or a person? Is it real or imagined? What do you want? Often the family member you are angry with is just in the wrong place at the wrong time. You may actually be angry about a decision your boss has made, the slow driver who made you late, or yourself for not handling a situation as well as you could have. It is usually safer to take out your anger on a spouse or child than other people – it is probably easier to yell at the children for not doing their homework than to face the possibility that you made a mistake. What alternative response could you use to get good results in handling this situation?

- **Reduce anger.** You might find that you are so angry that you can't resolve the problem until you cool down. Ask yourself what you can do to reduce your anger. Once you have a clearer idea of what is going on, take steps to change the anger-provoking situation. Put some humour into the situation to defuse the anger or hostility.

If you are experiencing anger, try to analyse the associated emotions for what they are: are they stimuli drawing on deep-seated subconscious feelings of anger that indicate unresolved emotional blocks from your past, or are they current anger issues which are playing on you? You also need to work out if, as I discovered, your anger is disproportionate to the precipitating event and determine if the event was nothing more than a trigger of deeply seated old anger over unresolved issues in your past.

In 1991, Dr David Spiegel stunned the medical community when lie reported that women with advanced breast cancer who went to support groups once a week in addition to their medical treatment had lived twice as long as other women with comparable cancer and medical care. No medical treatment at that point in the progression of the cancer could have helped as much. The women in these groups learned how to better handle the floods of fear and anger that can often overwhelm and exhaust people with cancer. One woman came in enraged, saying, 'Men are bastards.' What she really meant, she came to realise in talking with her group, was that she wanted her husband to be more caring while she went through chemotherapy. With that realisation, she was able to ask for and receive the care she really wanted.

Like that woman, some people discover they can make positive use of the energy or adrenalin released in anger to communicate with the other person or take action to solve a problem. There are different ways of dealing with situations that make you angry and everybody deals with things in different ways. Instead of lying awake angry all night, why not get up and plan a strategy to resolve a problem?

Anger and illness

I have often shown audiences on TV shows and in my seminars an intriguing demonstration of how emotional states can rapidly influence the body. As a volunteer subject, I will choose a man who seems to me to be strong and fit – often someone who regularly goes to the gym or practises weightlifting. I then ask him to think about something that makes him happy, loving, or generally positive and to hold the thought in his mind for about 30 seconds. I ask him to imagine that his physical body is absorbing this positive energy. When he has done this, I ask him to raise his left arm at 90 degrees from his body while I use all my strength to physically push his arm back down to his side again. Invariably, with a combination of positive thinking and his own physical strength, I find myself completely unable to move his arm from its outstretched position.

With both his arms now resting normally by the sides of his body, I then ask him to think of something that makes him really angry – it may be a person, a situation, even an injustice somewhere in the world. After focusing on anger for about 30 seconds and imagining it running through his body, I again ask him to raise his right arm to 90 degrees and try to physically push it back down to his side. Every time I have done this demonstration, the volunteer's arm has collapsed with ease back down to his side, all his strength seemingly sapped in seconds merely by thinking angry thoughts. It always brings a gasp of surprise from the volunteer and the audience, yet it is also an effect that I often see in my patients.

For example, Gordon, who was suffering from a brain tumour, found that the angrier he felt over his situation and the everyday tasks that he now had trouble in carrying out, the less energy he had and the more tired he felt. When he was relaxed and in a more positive frame of mind, his energy levels increased.

Robert was almost palpably angry following his diagnosis of multiple sclerosis. He would verbally lash out at his wife, make unpleasant remarks to almost anyone who enquired how he was feeling, and despair that he would ever walk properly again. He had come to believe that he was living only to experience pain and found this so physically and emotionally draining that he felt his life was becoming meaningless. He was angry and in deep despair. He eventually realised that he alone carried the responsibility of choice about how to react to his illness. He could let it control him, making him bitter, unhappy and increasingly friendless. Or he could choose to confront it with courage, and gain some control over his situation.

Robert chose to keep hope alive and to try to maintain a positive attitude. In so doing he was able to let go of his anger, assess his losses realistically and recognise that rebuilding a new life pattern involved first acceptance, then doing what had to be done in spite of his own vulnerability and no matter how overwhelming the odds might sometimes seem. 'The need to accept the things I cannot change, the courage to change the things I can, and the wisdom to know the difference, took on a new meaning for me.'

Over a long period of time, holding onto anger drains our energy and, as dozens of studies have shown, may potentially suppress our immune system against disease. It is not a matter of expressing our anger, and spitting like a snake at anyone who comes within range – it is important to learn how to communicate and manage anger in a socially responsible way. It also means that we don't keep a stiff upper lip and pretend to be placid when underneath we are seething. It is important to express anger constructively, as many of my patients have discovered. Anger can be an energising emotion, and a fuel for a fighting spirit – the opposite of despair and hopelessness.

If you have been diagnosed with a chronic illness, you have probably experienced shock and disbelief – 'How could this have happened to me?' There is anger – 'Why me?' Finally, there is acceptance that you will have to learn to live with this disease. While the shock and disbelief will probably fade as the reality of the illness sets in, the anger may remain. It may not be as strong as it was immediately after diagnosis, but it is likely to come in waves.

Many of my patients are only in their thirties when they receive the diagnosis of a serious or life-threatening illness. They often have to share this with young children. Frequently they have had to cut back or stop work altogether. Their independence is compromised. They sometimes find that medications don't work as well as they did, or don't work at all. Often they are angry at what they find to be an imperfect medical system and limited treatment options. In situations like this, you cannot control the fact that sometimes you *will* get angry. Sometimes situations will arise that can't be controlled and will put you on edge. However, you *can* control how you choose to use or channel that anger.

Anger is a natural emotional response to chronic illness. It ebbs and flows, becoming more dormant during certain stages and more prominent at others. It is most likely to surface when the illness is worsening. For some of my patients, everyday situations can become frustrating – getting in and out of a car, getting dressed, getting bathed, even having contact with friends. The more frustrated you become, the worse your symptoms are likely to become and the more likely anger is to set in. The loss of abilities and feelings of grief can both be triggers for anger. Anger is often a reaction to loss of ability and the horror of not being able to act the way you did before you became ill. It is a loss of health and independence, and grief over the loss of an expected future.

Uncertainty and fear can also lead to anger – a very large part of chronic illness is uncertainty. You don't know when, or if, certain symptoms and declines will occur; you don't know if that new drug will be ready for a trial that you may be able to take part in. Uncertainty can cause feelings of fear and helplessness that ignite anger and may have a detrimental effect on your health.

Although our reflex action is to discourage anger, to try to contain it or get rid of it altogether may not always be the best option. There can be benefits to anger as well. If you are seriously ill you may well find that your energy levels are severely depleted. A certain amount of frustration or anger can actually energise you. If anger is letting you object to something that is objectionable, it is helpful. If it is aiding you to be assertive when you need to be assertive, it is helpful. But if you are turning into an angry person who lashes out at those who are trying to help you, it is not useful. It would not be fair or entirely possible to deny yourself the painful and powerful emotion of anger. It is a part of who you are and you should express it. However, if you become stuck on this one emotion – which is easy to do – you may become entangled in it, unable to move beyond it. The key is to understand whether your anger is useful. Some therapists recommend that you allow anger to lead you to a connection within yourself that helps you to feel continuity with who you were before your illness.

For example, if you have excellent social skills you may feel upset and frustrated if your table manners begin to deteriorate as a result of your disease. One of my patients, Elisabeth, suffers from Parkinson's disease and is married to a high-flying husband involved in politics and fund-raising for charity. She has had to acknowledge that it takes emotional stamina to put herself in a situation where she may choose not to eat, but rather participate in conversation she finds of interest and value. She is still being herself as a social person.

Living in the present

One antidote to anger is learning to live in the present. If you are not stuck in the past or tormented by distant future images of what should be, you will have the opportunity to manage your day with awareness. Living in the moment with consciousness, patience, compassion and appreciation for yourself and others lets you proceed in a creative way, in spite of the pain and anger surrounding your losses. The goal is not necessarily to get anger out of your life. When you feel threatened, afraid or frustrated, anger is a normal response. However, you can also put your anger to work for you. It may be a signal that you need to take action. Anger can be a force for action, change and growth. The better you understand your anger, the better you will be able to use it for self-healing.

Exploring the roots of your relationship to anger

This exercise, when I used it in my seminars, helped numerous participants to manage and express anger in a positive way that did not involve blame or destructive outbursts. Some people found that the moment they took anger by the hand, what they thought was a big monster became a friendly one, or what they saw as a ball of fire shrank. Although many found that anger became some kind of cartoon character, they usually found that it changed quite dramatically as they went through the exercise. While it often began as an outsized, monstrous image, it became smaller and friendlier when taken by the hand, and smaller and friendlier still by the end of the exercise. If you learn to properly interpret anger, you can use your knowledge of its messages to communicate, to make changes, to right wrongs, or to rectify imbalances in your relationships.

Again, you can either read the following piece as you would an article, or you can ask a friend to read it for you. Alternatively, you may want to read it several times to yourself, pausing when it comes to breaks identified by a three-point ellipsis (...) in order to have time to experience that section in whatever way feels comfortable to you.

Sitting in a comfortable chair, imagine that you are walking through a beautiful field of long grass and meadow flowers. After taking in and enjoying this scene for a while, I'd like you to walk towards the edge of the field where a forest of tall oak, beech and fir trees begins. There is a small and quite narrow pathway leading into the depths of the forest and you begin to walk slowly down this track.

Eventually you find a cave – you stand and watch the entrance, wondering in an almost childlike way if anything lives inside it. To your surprise, stand and quietly watch as anger emerges from the cave. It can take on any form you like – it may be a person, an animal, a ball of fire, a mythical figure or anything else that symbolises anger. Let your imagination come up with any image of anger that feels right for you.

Imagine now that you approach your image of anger, and take it by the hand. You walk with it out of the forest and back into the beautiful, still, peaceful field. Sit down in the field with anger and hold a conversation with it. Find out about your anger with an open mind, willing to listen to whatever it may tell you. Perhaps, as a child, your anger protected you. Maybe it defended you from insults, ill-treatment or hurts. If you discover anger's protective quality, thank it for serving that purpose for you. Thank anger for being there for you.

Talk to anger about what it's done for you. Recognise that anger has protected you, but that you have other emotions and coping mechanisms that can also protect you now. As an adult you have other resources — assertiveness, control, articulation. Talk to anger about what it can and cannot do for you now.

When you have finished talking to anger, imagine that you stand up, walk back to the edge of the field, and bid goodbye to anger. Head back out into the field, but after a while turn around to see what has happened to anger. Did anger return to the cave, or is it still standing at the edge of the woods? Once you have an image of anger, continue on your way, walking across the field.

Chapter 6

Healing and Guilt

Guilt is the source of sorrows, the avenging fiend that follows us behind
with whips and stings. (Nicholas Rowe)

Guilt is probably the most common emotion that I see across a
wide range of my patients. For example, both Carol and Barbara
suffered greatly from feelings of guilt after being diagnosed with
lung cancer. Unfortunately, people who have lung cancer often face
something no other people with cancer face – blame. The blame
and guilt that many lung cancer sufferers are forced to deal with, on
top of all the other issues that go with a cancer diagnosis, comes
largely from the link between the disease and smoking. Since it has
become clear that smoking is harmful to health, the government,
the medical profession, and private individuals have strongly voiced
opposition to it. Unfortunately, negative feelings about smoking
sometimes spill over as negative feelings towards people who smoke
or have smoked. While it is true that smoking is bad for your health,
people who smoke or have smoked in the past are *not* bad people.

The blame and guilt for lung cancer can also come from within.
People with lung cancer often blame themselves. This is very
destructive and it can completely undermine your attempts to
adjust to your diagnosis. Guilt can lead to severe depression, which

in turn can make it nearly impossible for you to participate in treatment.

A group of researchers from Oxford University interviewed 45 patients with lung cancer about their illness. Their findings, published in 2004 in the *British Medical Journal*, showed that whether they smoked or not (some had never smoked), the patients felt stigmatised. They felt that they were blamed for their illness because of the general 'anti-smoking' climate in Britain. The feeling of guilt led to many people with lung cancer concealing their illness and not sharing their problems with doctors, family or friends.

I have other patients suffering from skin cancer, known as melanoma, who are wracked by guilt over the fact that they sat in the sun too long, didn't use a sufficiently high-factor sun cream, and ignored health warnings about the dangers of sunbathing.

A young couple, whose son I was treating, experienced overwhelming feelings of guilt after they discovered that his illness was caused by a hereditary disorder of which they were unaware. Unfortunately, many parents in a similar situation only learn about these rare genetic diseases after reading lots of articles and talking to expert doctors. 'Even though intellectually we know that we can't control everything, we still feel that we should have prevented our child's illness. We feel so guilty because of the gap between what we think we *should* be able to do and control, and what we *actually* can control and achieve as parents,' they told me.

As parents we are often hard on ourselves. You may have to learn how to forgive yourself for not being 'perfect and all-knowing'. Feeling guilty over the illness, and maybe the death, of a child is very common and very pervasive for parents. In order to cope with these feelings it is very important to first confront them and admit that they exist. In many cases, moving through guilt can evoke other intense feelings that must be dealt with in order to have some sense of healing.

Sometimes I have a patient who has been told that the connection between body, mind and spirit is so strong that by imagining the white blood cells attacking the diseased cells, their cancer will disappear. An inappropriate and unhealthy feeling of guilt for not having prayed hard enough or willed strongly enough can surface when physical healing does not occur. In each case, guilt overwhelms and is detrimental to the recovery process.

The simple fact is that illnesses are caused and affected by a combination of genetic, biological, environmental, behavioural and psychosocial factors. Even the most optimistic, positive, giving and loving people with excellent mental health fall victim to serious illness. As we have discovered in this book, while there is considerable data to support the positive impact that healthy attitudes and behaviours have on reducing the risk of illness, the biology of disease can be overwhelming.

In responding to a patient's feelings of guilt, I have to be non-judgemental in a caring way. Some patients find it helpful if I can reflect their feelings, offer insight, or share my experience of similar circumstances. Often they are looking for validation to be able to accept themselves for who they are. They sometimes need to be challenged to stop living in the past and start looking to the future – to see that perhaps even without a cure, there are healthy ways to live with a disease.

The meaning of guilt

Rarely has one word – guilt – been so widely misunderstood. It is often viewed as a virtue, as a high sense of responsibility and morality. However, the truth is that guilt is the greatest destroyer of emotional energy. It leaves you feeling immobilised in the present by something that occurred in the past. Of course, we need to have a conscience because without one we would have no compunction about hurting each other, and the world would be an even less safe place. When your conscience tells you that you have done something wrong, it is important to face it, make amends and learn from your mistake. Staying consumed with guilt will keep you from moving forward in a positive and productive way.

As a society, we seem to be consumed by guilt, or at least with trying to eliminate it from our lives. A search of a major online bookseller's website for the word 'guilt' results in over 500 titles! You can cook without guilt, diet without guilt, eat chocolate or fried foods without guilt, be a guilt-free working parent or a guilt-free single parent, and a guilt-free golfer. Maybe you want to recognise guilt, understand guilt, overcome guilt, be liberated from guilt, or put an end to guilt.

Webster's Dictionary defines guilt as:

- the fact of being responsible for wrongdoing or a crime

- a feeling of responsibility for having done something wrong

Guilt is the inability to forgive yourself for a perceived wrongdoing. *Perceived wrongdoing* means that you *believe* you have done something wrong. It may or may not have had negative consequences for yourself or someone else. If others were involved, they may or may not still be angry or hurt by the wrongdoing. A perceived wrongdoing may be an action or lack of action, a thought or a feeling. If the wrongdoing was an action, you probably think of it as a mistake. You feel guilty for it because you neither forgive yourself for it, nor let it go. If you cannot forgive yourself, you will probably have difficulty in overcoming your guilt. We have all felt guilty at one time or another, but some people feel guilty most of the time. If they make a mistake, they never forget it and feel badly about it.

In fact, there are several types of guilt. You can feel ashamed, unworthy or embarrassed about actions for which you are responsible – this is known as 'true guilt' or guilt that is appropriate. However, you can also feel guilty about events for which you are not responsible. This 'false guilt' can be equally destructive, if not more so. Feeling guilty for events that are out of your control is unproductive and detrimental.

Shame is an emotion closely related to guilt, but it is important to understand the differences. According to *Webster's Dictionary,* shame can be defined as 'a painful emotion caused by consciousness of guilt, shortcoming or impropriety'. It has also been said that we feel guilty for what we *do,* but we feel shame for what we *are.*

Guilt and lifestyle

We are told that in order to deal with the stresses of our everyday life, we should take more time to enjoy the health benefits from doing the things we most enjoy. Indeed, I have advocated this in many parts of this book. Yet, according to a recent research study, over 40 per cent of people in Britain would enjoy their everyday pleasures more if they did not feel so guilty! Scientists know that enjoyment relieves stress and enhances our immune system, but now say that needless guilt reduces this enjoyment as well as our quality of life, undermining both mental and physical health. A British research group, Associates for Research Into the Science of Enjoyment (ARISE), were the first to study the relationship between pleasure and guilt. They looked at attitudes in eight countries to 13 everyday pleasures including having a glass of wine, a cigarette, a piece of chocolate, tea or coffee, watching TV, or sex.

- The British came second in the overall international 'pleasure league', but they are above average when it comes to feeling guilty afterwards, a contradiction the researchers say could be bad for our health.

- The Dutch have the most relaxed attitude to pleasure. They enjoy themselves more than anyone else and do not get bogged down in the guilt trap.

• The Germans rank bottom of the league for enjoyment and when they do let themselves go, they feel guiltier than anyone else in Europe.

Professor David Warburton, founder of ARISE and Head of Psychopharmacology at the University of Reading, believes that guilt acts as an important social check on personal behaviour, for example preventing people committing crime. However, it can be misplaced when it is related to lifestyle. In its extreme, guilt can impair attentiveness, making people forgetful and more prone to error, he says. Chronic guilt, he claims, can induce stress and depression which can lead to eating disorders and contribute to infection, ulcers, heart problems and even brain damage. He found that a number of common pleasures attract high levels of guilt, perhaps reflecting the way that health campaigns such as we are now seeing in Britain have affected the way people view their pleasures. Health campaigns often send conflicting messages. It is interesting that the survey conducted by ARISE shows that one in two people (51 per cent) resent authorities constantly telling them what is good and bad for them.

Conversely, few people feel guilty about enjoying sex or listening to music, both of which have very high pleasure ratings. In spite of feeling guilty about their pleasures, most people do little about it. One in three simply carries the burden of guilt with them as part of life.

Laboratory studies show that people choose their pleasures in a rational and deliberate way designed to enhance their quality of life in any given circumstances. A favourite treat, such as a cup of tea or coffee, a glass of wine or beer, or a bar of chocolate reduces stress and helps you to relax. If you get caught in the guilt trap your choices become distorted and you then either sacrifice your enjoyment or live with the guilt. This in turn can undermine the positive benefits of enjoyment that countless studies show can protect you against stress and strengthen your immune system.

Aldous Huxley warned us in *Brave New World* of a time when humankind's almost infinite appetite for distractions is used as a means of control by, in effect, inflicting pleasure. Today, Huxley's nightmare is in danger of becoming a reality.

The conflict between the lifestyle we have and the one we feel we should have has been investigated in research which shows significant differences between the 'real' and the 'ideal' self. It shows that the ideal self is perceived as significantly more alert, slimmer and fitter. It eats more 'healthy' food and less 'unhealthy' food. It is more attractive and generally more desirable than the real self. Living up to the internal expectations of the 'ideal self' can be a major source of stress and cause guilt for most people. This can be made worse by calls to change our lifestyles, which can increase the gulf between the real self and the ideal self. It is interesting to note that the top items in the guilt division (eating sweet things, fatty foods, chocolate, lack of exercise and smoking) have all featured as targets of health campaigns.

It has long been known that guilt is a source of chronic mental disorders, and it is frequently associated with depression. Indeed, the link is so well accepted that measures of guilt are also used as indices of depression. Thus, 'excessive or inappropriate guilt' is one of the nine clinical criteria used to diagnose major depression. Chronic feelings of unresolved guilt can spiral, providing an endless reminder of the failing that originally caused the guilt.

Guilt-induced depression can result in eating disorders, of which self-punishment is often a component. In turn this can lead to a vicious spiral in which people with bulimia – which is characterised by binge eating – often try to alleviate their guilt by making themselves vomit, starving themselves, or exercising compulsively. They then try to cheer themselves up by bingeing, and the spiral continues: depression – bingeing – guilt – vomiting – self-loathing – depression – bingeing.

When you're made to feel guilty

There are times when people use guilt to try to manipulate us into doing things they want us to do. There may also be times when we do the same thing. Guilt can be a useful tool for helping you to reflect on your motivations and on your relationships with others. It can also be useful in helping you to recognise when you are being manipulated. It is important to develop a sense of self-awareness so that you can see those guilty little red flags when they appear and be aware of your behaviour, enabling you to gauge whether you are responding out of guilt or from a genuine desire to help. If you feel someone is pushing your guilt buttons to achieve their own ends, ask yourself whether their request is reasonable. If not, address the issue with them directly. Tell them they are not being fair and express your feelings in an honest way. Don't resort to doing what they ask if you feel it is inappropriate because that breeds resentment. If you find yourself unable to confront others when you are feeling manipulated, or if you are feeling overwhelmed by guilty feelings that you can't pinpoint or resolve, you might find it helpful to seek professional help. To help you distinguish what is right for you to do because you are guilt ridden, I would suggest:

- Don't let others' values dictate the way you live your life. Decide for yourself what is important to you, what you value, or the way you wish to be.

- Don't expect to be pleasant, wise and even-tempered at all times. It is normal to feel irritable or angry occasionally. Feeling guilty about negative emotions is futile.

- Forgive yourself for mistakes in judgement. Learn something from your mistakes. Make them work for you in the future.

• Take satisfaction in your accomplishments, rather than dwelling on your shortcomings.

Guilt and health

Chronic guilt can increase levels of stress hormones, potentially leading to infection, cardiovascular and gastro-intestinal problems, even possibly brain damage. Human stress hormones such as cortisol, adrenalin and noradrenalin are essential for surviving acute physical stress, but they can cause adverse effects (such as infection, ulcers, and heart disease) when secretion is sustained. Cortisol has been implicated in causing brain damage. Sustained levels of cortisol secretion, resulting from chronic guilt, can decay the hippocampus, a part of our brain responsible for cognitive functions such as memory. Loss of hippocampus has also been found in patients with Cushing's syndrome, which is characterised by overproduction of cortisol and can lead to depression, baldness, diabetes and facial hair growth, even among women.

A team of researchers from Hull University asked students to list their favourite activities, giving them both a pleasure and a guilt rating from 1 to 10. Samples of saliva from the participants were then tested for levels of S-Iga (immunoglobulin A), an antibody which is the body's first line of defence against infection. They found that high guilt ratings were accompanied by low immunoglobulin levels.

Another scientific study reported in 2004 by researchers at the University of California, showed that shame and guilt can affect the immune system and inflammatory products in the body. Healthy participants were randomly assigned during three 20-minute experimental laboratory sessions over one week to write either about traumatic experiences in which they blamed themselves, or about neutral experiences. Those participants who reported the greatest increases in shame and guilt in response to the task showed the greatest increases in pro-inflammatory cytokine activity which weakened their immunity.

As a healer, I have found that the greatest levels of guilt and shame are often experienced by those who are diagnosed HIV positive. In the mid-1980s I found myself being pilloried by a vociferous minority of people who thought that I should not be trying to help AIDS and HIV sufferers. The tabloids were publishing stories about the 'gay plague' and quoting moralisers who saw the illness as divine retribution for a degenerate and promiscuous lifestyle. The hostility and fear that HIV/AIDS provoked in the general population is now a memory, but in the 1980s it was as large a component in treatment as the virus itself. Many people still feel shame and guilt because they are made to believe that they must have done something wrong or immoral in order to be infected with HIV. Combating the virus effectively, as many studies have now shown, involves reducing stress that can weaken the immune system.

One of my patients confided at the time: 'People stand up in the pulpit and denounce you, shun you and don't want to know. They don't want to help. There are very few hands willing to hold yours.' At that time the stigma attached to the virus could overtake the effort to fight it. With the support of his wife, that man did not act on his initial impulse to hang himself and eventually succeeded in overcoming his shock, fear and guilt. He came to believe in his own powers of healing and redefined his approach to life. 'I think peace of mind will definitely prevent my health deteriorating. I have every chance of surviving and I cannot see any reason for not surviving. I am not under stress. I am perfectly calm and nothing is going to worry me.' Almost 25 years after first becoming infected, he still visits me regularly for healing and his health has not deteriorated.

Overcoming guilt

Myths about guilt abound, but two of the most common are that guilt is a valuable exercise from which you will learn and grow, and that if you consume yourself with guilt you won't make the same mistake again. However, while reflecting on past behaviour and learning from it is instructive, unending remorse about past mistakes serves no useful purpose. In fact, excessive guilt is one of the greatest destroyers of self-esteem and personal development.

So what is the best way to stop yourself feeling guilty? What can you do with guilt you definitely deserve, but which can no longer do you any good? When I have asked some of my patients this question, there were four predominating suggestions:

1. **Recognise that some guilt feelings are good for you.**
   Therapy that focuses on 'feeling good' may ensure that you will repeat your mistakes, especially when dealing with other people. One of my patients, a psychotherapist specialising in addictions, makes a point of not relieving the guilt of practising alcoholics, because they have to learn the consequences of their actions before they can be motivated to change. Someone once said the role of a therapist is to comfort the afflicted and afflict the comforted!

2. **Examine the cause of self-generated guilt.** In doing so, you can avoid putting yourself into situations that might, once again, create guilt.

3. **Acknowledge to others that you have made a mistake.** Even though 'I made a mistake' and 'I'm sorry' are two of the shortest sentences in the English language, they are also two of the most difficult for many people to speak. When you have the courage to use them, they are extremely healing for both the person saying the words and the one listening.

4. **Forgive yourself.** Learning how to do this is not nearly as difficult as you might think. Once you have practised it a few

times, you will almost certainly find that releasing guilt is one of the greatest gifts you can give yourself.

Forgiving yourself

Bruce, another of my patients infected with HIV, found that forgiveness was a crucial tool in dealing with the guilt he experienced after he had tested HIV positive.

> The guilt was enormous. I was losing my future by torturing myself over my past behaviour, over mistakes. Mistakes. They sound so innocent, yet their power to subjugate me under their spell was enormous.
>
> Maybe I was using my guilt to shield myself from reality, or to delay having to accept responsibility for my own future, because I was too busy lamenting the past. I seemed to be unable to move past those mistakes or the guilt they inspired. I had yet to learn about the true power of forgiveness. How sad that it took me far too many years to realise that I alone held the key to my forgiveness.
>
> Forgiveness is moving on. It is recognising all that you have lost because of your refusal to forgive yourself. It is realising that the energy that you spent hanging on to the past is better spent on attaining your future. You must let go of the past, so that you can reach for your future. You are moving on – not attempting to change the past. Holding on to guilt serves no good purpose as it just drains your being. Forgiveness is one of the greatest gifts you can give yourself.

We all need to learn that making mistakes is an important part of life. Mistakes are a tool for learning. When you think about the cause of your guilt, consider what you have learned from it. If you feel you haven't learned anything, what can you learn now? Are you having trouble forgiving yourself because you expect yourself to be perfect? If someone else made the same mistake, what would you

tell them? You probably won't overcome guilt in a day. Imagine your
life without guilt. Imagine how you would feel about yourself if you
did not regret your mistakes. Practise letting go. Practise acceptance.
Practise forgiveness.

A forgiveness meditation

If your heart has become burdened with anger and
resentment about someone – especially if that someone is
you – it's probably time that you found a way to release the
weight of anger and guilt you've been carrying and get on
with your life. You have better things to do! If you have been
carrying a heavy burden of guilt over something that
happened a long time ago – or maybe just last month – you
may well find the following exercise helps you to release that
guilt. You can use it in several different ways: you may simply
want to read it as you would any article, with the purpose of
learning something and exploring how it might apply to
you; alternatively, you may want to get back into the past
more deeply by reading it several times to yourself, pausing
when it comes to breaks identified by a three-point ellipsis
(...) in order to have time to experience that section in
whatever way feels comfortable to you. Or you can first
speak it into a tape recorder (or have a friend read it for you,
or buy my CD) and then, as you listen to it, close your eyes
and follow along in whatever way feels right to you.

*You can begin this meditation by first becoming as comfortable as
you can ... and as you allow yourself to relax and your body to feel
fully supported, gently close your eyes. Turn your attention to your
breath, first focusing for a while on the outgoing breaths, feeling the
air leaving your body ... and then, for a while, experiencing the
breaths you breath in ... with each breath allowing yourself to*

*become more and more relaxed, more and more comfortable . . .
Remaining very relaxed and yet alert, quieten the chatter in your
mind and become aware of that place within where you are open to
healing and new possibilities . . .*

*And now, from that centred, open place within, remember something
you did, or failed to do, that causes you to feel bad when you are
reminded of it . . . As you remember the mistake you criticise yourself
for, experience the guilt and pain you have carried in your heart
because you made decisions back then that you later wished you
hadn't made . . .*

*Allow an image to form of who you were when you made decisions
you now regret. Have this image stand or sit in front of you and
experience as fully as you can what you looked like back then, even
what you would have worn . . .*

*As you observe this person that you once were, recall your former
goals, your dreams, your expectations . . . What experiences had you
that created your outlook on life? . . . Notice how much less you knew
then and how much more you still needed to learn about life . . .*

*When you made this mistake, were you determined to mess up your
life or to harm someone else? If you knew how to make better
choices, did you deliberately make wrong ones? The answer, of course,
is 'no'. How do you make your choices today? You try to do the best
you can, even though in the future, you'll learn even more things it
would be helpful to know right now. We all have to make our
decisions based on the experience and knowledge we currently have.
You do not plan to make poor choices.*

*Unfortunately, when you think about who you were back then, you
condemn yourself for not making good choices. The regret you feel gets*

piled together with the guilt from other mistakes you've made until you carry a very heavy load. Fortunately, you can lighten that load of guilt by no longer demanding that the younger version of yourself should have known what you could not possibly have known at that time.

And so, again bring your attention to the image of yourself as you were in the past. As you are looking at this younger self, I will read you some words you can use to release the guilt you've been carrying. I will first go through this statement without any pauses and will then read the words again more slowly, giving you time to repeat the words either aloud or silently to yourself. You may want to say the same words I say or, if you prefer, choose words that are more comfortable for you. There will be times when you will need to add your own words in order to make this exercise fit your specific situation.

Here is what you can now say to the person you used to be:

When I look back on what you did or did not do, I have a difficult time accepting you. I expected you to make choices you did not know how to make. I expected you to do things you did not know how to do. Those expectations have made me very critical of you. I wanted you to be different from who you were. Now I am willing to remove the conditions I placed on you to be someone you could not be at the time. I remove the demands and expectations that have kept me from accepting you. My love and affection go out to you just as you are.

Now I will repeat those words again and you may follow in any way you would like. Again, remember that you can change any words if you wish or may use the words just as you hear them ... Looking at the person you used to be, you say:

When I look back on what you did or did not do ... I have a difficult time accepting you ... I expected you to make choices you did not know how to make ... I expected you to do things you did not know how to do ... Those expectations have made me very critical of you ... Now I am willing to remove the conditions I placed on you to be someone you could not be at the time ... I remove the demands and expectations that have kept me from accepting you ... My love and affection go out to you just as you are ...

And now, feel love flowing from you to the image of the younger person you carry inside, the one who was doing the best he or she could do at the time mistakes were made. As you do, allow yourself to be both the giver and receiver of forgiveness, letting that love flow through every part of your body . . . Feel the release of tension that comes from forgiveness . . .

Imagine now a symbol that represents your willingness to forgive yourself. It may be something tangible, a real object that you can experience with your senses. Or perhaps it's an intangible symbol, like a peaceful ocean breeze or a sunrise that might symbolise forgiveness ... Receive this symbol as a gift you give yourself, noticing how you might use it to reinforce your new view of yourself ...

Now, in the final part of this exercise, notice if there is a small step you can take to demonstrate that you love and accept yourself just as you are – and as you were, even while striving to be a better person . . .

And now, become aware of the room, bringing with you whatever is important for you to remember... Taking a deep breath ... stretch your arms and legs ... and gently open your eyes so that you are fully alert and awake, appreciating all you have learned and who you have become.

Chapter 7
Healing and Guided Imagery

> We are what we are imagine. Our very existence consists in our
> imagination of ourselves ... The greatest tragedy that can befall us is to
> go unimagined. (N. Scott Momaday, Native American)

From the earliest point in my work as a healer I have used guided imagery – or what I used to call visualisation. As a child I spent much of my time daydreaming and in an inner space that no one else could reach. Maybe that was the first inkling that in later life I was going to follow a rather unusual career path. I never thought much about what was, for me, a natural talent. It was only years later when I participated in scientific research that I was asked what I was doing as I sat with my eyes closed and my hands close to a test tube of enzymes, blood cells or cancer cells.

A particularly striking example of the sort of guided imagery I used came from an intriguing experiment in which I took part at the University of California in the 1970s. It was conducted by Dr Fred Lorenz, Professor Emeritus of the Department of Animal Physiology at Davis. He was interested to discover whether I could influence someone from a distance, and if so, whether it could be seen in the brainwave patterns of the subject.

Professor Lorenz himself was keen to be my first subject. He sat in an isolation room with his eyes closed while I sat in an adjacent room unable to see him. Both of us had electrodes attached to our scalps and connected to an electroencephalograph (EEG) machine. This recorded the information picked up by each electrode. The pattern created by all the individual traces shows the state of consciousness of the person to whom the electrodes are attached. I was given instructions by another of the researchers to either arouse or sedate Lorenz. A clear result was achieved, both according to the readout from the EEG and from Lorenz's own recollection of what he experienced. He said that he was

> very aware of being alerted three times, with drowsy or inattentive periods between ... My first remembered alerting was most dramatic and seemed to come out of drowsiness or even actual sleep.
>
> The correspondences between Matthew's EEG and my own were most dramatic. These are most clearly illustrated by moments such as those where trains of high amplitude or slow waves are simultaneously evident from both our heads. Especially interesting was a kappa rhythm which manifested simultaneously in both heads. The kappa rhythm is usually a sign of alerting during a drowsy state.
>
> The correspondence was not limited to such short-term and striking displays. It seemed that usually when Matthew was producing alpha rhythm, so was I. There were three consecutive pages of an awakened period – i.e., they cover 30 seconds of record. During that half-minute Matthew's record and mine shifted simultaneously from low amplitude, fast beta to irregular slow waves and then back to quite regular alpha. Such correspondences could be seen throughout the record.

Professor Lorenz and his colleagues were intrigued to know what I had been doing mentally to demonstrate this effect. It was simple.

When asked to 'sedate' Lorenz for a 30-second period, I had been imagining and visualising him deeply relaxed and asleep. The image had been very clear in my mind and I had been trying to somehow transmit it to him from one room to another. However, when I had been asked to arouse him I imagined that I was running into his room, shouting to him that the building was on fire and that he had to get out quickly! Not only had he somehow 'felt' the effects of my imagery, they had also shown clearly on the EEG readout from both of our brains.

Later on, in my seminars, I would demonstrate to participants numerous examples of guided imagery which similarly affected their bodies. Think, for example, of holding a fresh, juicy lemon in your hand. Perhaps you can feel its texture and the vividness of its yellow skin. As you start to peel it, some of the juice squirts out. You can really smell the aroma of the fruit – it's very strong. Now, put the lemon in your mouth, suck on it, and taste the lemon juice as it rolls over your tongue. Almost certainly, like the great majority of those in my seminars, your mouth will start watering. If you can activate your saliva glands by thinking about a lemon, why should you not be able to create reactions in other parts of your body by using imagery? Ironically, simple mind–body techniques like those I was demonstrating 30 years ago have now become the focus of widespread research with great implications for medicine and healing.

Visualisation and physiology

Recent advances in medical technology have allowed researchers to watch blood flow changes to different parts of the brain by the use of sophisticated imaging equipment called PET (Positron Emission Tomography) scanners. It is now known that the same parts of the brain are activated regardless of whether you actually experience something or vividly imagine it. In other words, picturing an image of a beautiful sunset activates the same area of the cerebral cortex as actually seeing a beautiful sunset. Listening to your favourite music triggers the same area of your brain as does imagining the music in your mind. Imagining the touch of a cotton shirt warm from the drier activates the same area of your brain as feeling the warm touch on your skin.

This helps us to understand how guided imagery can influence your physical body and your biochemistry. Vivid imagery stimulates the same brain centres as the 'real thing', in turn sending messages to your limbic system (the 'feeling centre' of your brain), your autonomic nervous system (which controls bodily functions such as heart rate, blood pressure, perspiration, respiratory rate, etc.), and your endocrine system (the control centre for all your hormones, including stress hormones such as cortisol and adrenalin). Everyone knows what it is like to wake from a really frightening dream when you find your heart pounding, your muscles aching, your breathing quickened and your skin sweating. This is the power of the 'imaginary' world of visualisation and imagery.

Of course, visualisation is not limited solely to health promotion. It has also been widely used by sportspeople. For example, Swiss triathlete Brigitte McMahon said that she had visualised the final sprint to the finish in her mind many times before coming to the Olympic Games in Australia in 2000. She claims the technique gave her the advantage because she was already prepared for it – had, in fact, planned the outcome already – in her mind. An athlete will create images, like pictures or movies, that recreate their best performances, or they will envision a desired outcome. While imagining these scenarios, the athlete imagines every detail and the way it feels to perform just the way they want. These images can be visual (images and pictures), kinaesthetic (how the body may feel), or auditory (McMahon reported imagining the roar of the crowd). (Musicians may find that sounds are more powerful than visual images, chefs will prefer smells, and dancers may best conjure up physical motions.) Using the mind, an athlete can call up these images over and over, enhancing the skill through repetition or rehearsal, similar to physical practice. With mental rehearsal, minds and bodies become trained to actually perform the skill imagined. Guided imagery and visualisation can maximise the effectiveness of an athlete's training. In a world where sports performance and success is measured in one-hundredths of a second, most athletes will use every possible training technique available. Jack Nicklaus, the golfer, attributes 50 per cent of his success to the mental imagery he uses before he takes each stroke. Visualisation is used by many to gain that very slim margin.

Visualisation takes advantage of what might almost be termed a 'weakness' of the body, in so far as it is unable to differentiate between a vivid mental experience and an actual physical experience. Charles Garfield, a psychologist, world-class athlete and computer scientist who has worked with NASA, has been one of the leading figures in the study of visualisation, which he also links to 'peak performance'. He says that he first heard that phrase from a cancer patient, a nationally known concert pianist who said, 'Staying alive these days is my peak performance.' Garfield later studied cancer survivors at the University of California Medical Center in San Francisco and concluded that most of them had the ability to enter states of mind that enabled their bodies to perform, like those of athletes, at levels beyond the ordinary.

In the early phases of the American space programme NASA scientists predicted that during prolonged lunar space flights, astronauts would experience irregular blood pressure and heart rate. To combat these effects, rather than risk drugs that had never been tested at zero gravity, the astronauts were taught how to pre-programme their minds and bodies with guided imagery for optimal space performance. What was learned from these space projects – the use of visualisation and biofeedback – also contributed to the investigations of mind–body medicine.

One basic premise of mind–body medicine is that all your thoughts and feelings are chemical. When you imagine a soothing walk along a warm sandy beach – a vivid thought and feeling – your body produces neuropeptides, chemical messengers for those thoughts and feelings. They in turn circulate throughout your body, exerting their influence and spreading their message to the cells of your immune system, nervous system and endocrine system. Your body then converts your ideas and expectations into biochemical realities. When properly harnessed, you can utilise appropriate ideas and instructions to help activate and augment your own healing system.

In the late 1970s, guided imagery was first popularised as a treatment for cancer patients by oncologist Carl Simonton and his psychologist wife, Stephanie. They had developed a programme for cancer patients using conventional treatment and visualisation. Dr Simonton noticed that patients who experienced spontaneous remission of cancer were usually those who said, 'I always imagined myself as well.' The programme involved a method of guided imagery in which patients imagined their white blood cells, or their chemotherapy drugs, destroying their cancer cells. The white cells or drugs would be imagined as saviours on white horses or heroic warriors – any image that conjured up strength and ruthless efficiency against the cancer cells, which would be seen as confused or weak. Patients would visualise the heroic cells or drugs attacking and overwhelming the less powerful cancer cells. The classic guided image used by the Simontons in their early work was one where each of the patient's white blood cells was the old video game character Pac-Man, and that they went out to gobble up bacteria, viruses and cancer cells.

Their research produced promising data suggesting that cancer patients who used guided imagery, along with psychotherapy and other supportive treatments, could outlive their doctors' expectations for their survival. Some of their scientific methods have subsequently been questioned, and the idea that visualisation can be used to fight cancer directly remains a complex and controversial one. What has been clearly demonstrated is that guided imagery can lessen the side-effects of chemotherapy and reduce pain in cancer patients. But, if guided imagery can make you relax, feel more positive and comforted, and less scared, then that alone is of great value.

Although the Simontons' work with guided imagery and cancer fired the public imagination, it has yet to be proved that visualisation can be relied upon to cure serious diseases like cancer or heart disease. However, hundreds of reports in medical journals now show just how effective guided imagery can be with other health conditions.

Guided imagery and medical research

- A 1996 study at the Cleveland Clinic showed that patients who used guided imagery prior to colorectal surgery had less anxiety before and less pain after the surgery than did the control group. The members of the guided imagery group used 37 per cent less pain medication, regained their bowel function sooner, and were released from the hospital an average of a day and a half earlier. Blue Shield of California (a health insurance company) has even started to distribute guided imagery recordings to its members scheduled for major surgery in the hope that the practice will decrease surgical complications and the pain and anxiety associated with surgery – as well as, presumably, saving the company money! The results of this study have been repeated several times and reported in medical journals.

- In a series of studies, Karen Olness and her colleagues demonstrated that, with practice, people could learn to control at least one aspect of their immune function. Subjects were taught to induce a relaxed state of well-being. They were then instructed to create an image of neutrophils, one type of white blood cell important in the defence against bacterial or fungal infection and thought to be important in autoimmune disease such as inflammatory arthritis. For example, one subject imagined her neutrophils as table-tennis balls with honey oozing out onto their surface, causing them to stick to everything they touched. When their blood samples were tested, it was found that subjects who practised relaxation and guided imagery exercises were able to selectively increase the stickiness of their neutrophils.

• A study by Dr Henry Bennett, a leading pioneer and researcher in the field of behavioural anaesthesia, examined the effect of simple preoperative instructions in decreasing blood loss during spinal surgery. Surgical procedures involving fusions or instrumentation of the spine are usually bloody, often requiring transfusions. In this particular study, 94 patients scheduled for spinal surgery were randomly assigned to one of three groups, all of which received a 15-minute talk from a psychologist. The first group was given information about neurological monitoring during spinal surgery. The second group was taught about neurological monitoring and was also taught to relax its muscles during the operation. The third group received all of these instructions, *plus* specific directions for moving blood away from the surgical incision site during the operation (in order to minimise blood loss) and then moving blood back towards the site afterwards, in order to maximise wound healing. The findings showed that patients in this last group were able to exert positive mental control over their blood loss during surgery. They lost an average of 500cc of blood compared to 900cc of blood loss in the first and second groups. These results held true even after controlling for the length of incision and the length of time under anaesthesia.

- Psychiatrist Dr Richard Smith, of the University of Arkansas, carried out a study in which he injected a woman under the arm with a chicken-pox virus; she had previously had chicken-pox and so had a natural defence mechanism against it. The resulting swelling at the site of the injection and its later disappearance was the expected result for someone whose immune system was working well against the virus. This was confirmed by a blood test showing an increase in her white blood cells responding to the virus. Over each of the next three weeks, she was injected again and instructed each time to use guided imagery to reduce the swelling. The result was a smaller swelling with each subsequent injection and a corresponding reduction in the white blood cell count required to deal with the virus. Finally, the woman was instructed to return her immune system to normal. Further injections resulted in a repeat of the original response. The experiment showed that guided imagery could have an effect on the immune system.

- A group of metastasic cancer patients using daily guided imagery for a year achieved significant improvements in natural killer cell activity and several other measures of immune functioning. Researchers in Denmark also found increased natural killer cell activity among college students who imagined their immune systems becoming very effective. Another group of researchers at Ohio State University found that people with cancer who used guided imagery while receiving chemotherapy felt more relaxed, better prepared for their treatment and more positive about care than those who didn't use the technique.

- In a controlled study, 55 mothers of infants in a neonatal intensive care unit were examined for the effects of relaxation and guided imagery on breast milk production. They received a 20-minute audiotape of progressive relaxation followed by guided imagery of pleasant surroundings, milk flowing in the breasts, and the baby's warm skin against theirs. They produced more than twice as much milk in comparison with those receiving only routine care.

• For those in pursuit of the safest sex possible, Dr Beverly Whipple of the State University of New Jersey published a report called 'Physiological Correlatives of Imagery-Induced Orgasm in Women' in the *Archives of Sexual Behaviour.* She studied women who claimed they could experience orgasm from imagery alone. Sitting stationary in a chair with their hands behind their backs, they were able to bring themselves to physical sexual climax purely through their own thought processes. The imagery-induced orgasm was measurably as strong – in terms of heart rate, systolic blood pressure, and pupil diameter – as the more conventional variety.

Few of us are educated in the use of the imagination, although – as we have now seen – it is one of our most powerful mental functions. Our educational system is geared towards teaching us logical, linear thinking. While this is invaluable in life, we are generally discouraged from using too much imagination and are rarely trained in how to focus it and use it well. Fortunately, we use imagination instinctively, since it is a normal, natural way for our brains and nervous systems to store, process and retrieve information.

Imagination is important in healing because it seems to have a much more direct link to bodily functions than spoken words. Imagery involves employing thoughts that have sensory qualities – what you see, hear, smell or feel inside. The power of imagination is closely linked to healing. When you shift your state of being from one that is anxious, depressed or uncomfortable, to one that is quieter, happier and more comfortable, physiological changes accompany this shift. The calmer, more relaxed and yet often more energised state that follows is one often associated with healing. It allows your body to focus its attention on healing rather than spending its energy combating imagined worries and problems.

Diana, a delightful patient of mine who suffers from rheumatoid arthritis, finds that using her imagination helps her to cope with high levels of pain. As she explains:

> Does healing mean that if I am an amputee missing a limb and it regrows, making me physically whole again, I am considered healed? I know that if you have a debilitating or deforming illness, you can overcome the pain barrier by stepping 'out of the box' and defeating the normal bodily response to pain and debilitation. This in turn makes it easier to step 'out of the box' on other levels. One of the ways I do this is by using my ability to daydream and enter a world beyond the confines of my body where nothing is impossible ...

Learning the basics of guided imagery

I believe that almost anyone can successfully use imagery. It is a question of patience and persistence, like learning to play a musical instrument. How long it will take before you begin to see results depends on the seriousness of your ailment, the vividness of your imagery and your own determination. If you have a sprained ankle, you may get relief in just one five-minute session, while it may take weeks for a person with severe burns to notice any significant pain reduction. I suggest that initially you practise your imagery for 15 to 20 minutes a day to ensure that you are learning to do it properly. As you become more skilled and comfortable with the technique, you'll be able to do it for just a few minutes at a time as needed throughout the day.

I have always found that the most effective images are those that have some meaning to you. However, one of my patients imagined his cancer cells as shrivelled pieces of fruit and his healthy cells as plump juicy berries. He pictured his immune system as birds that would fly in and pick up and carry away the raisin-like cells, allowing the rest of the cells to flourish.

Guided imagery comes much more naturally to children. In my experience they respond to it easily because they haven't had time to be educated away from this natural, innate ability. Music, when carefully chosen, will increase the effects of imagery. On one occasion I was playing the album *Oxygene* by Jean-Michel Jarre to a youngster with cancer. Inspired by the synthesised laser-like sounds of the music, he imagined his immune cells as silver bullets coming in and destroying his cancer cells.

One important reason that it is helpful to try to create your own images is that they relate to the deeply personal aspect of visualisation. For example, one person's beautiful beach scene may be another person's nightmare. The person who suffers from hay fever may not find it comfortable to imagine themselves in a grassy spring meadow. If you are trying to experience inner peace, you must conjure up images that are peaceful to you.

If you find visualisation difficult, don't judge yourself – remember that not everyone sees pictures clearly in their mind's eye. One simple method that may help you if you are experiencing difficulties in transporting yourself to imaginary scenes involves first imagining yourself on a magic carpet which takes you to that special place of peace and serenity. It can evoke the magical childhood belief in limitless possibilities.

Once you have found a peaceful inner place, you can then visualise more specific images based on the kind of pictures that seem to have the strongest healing potential for different conditions. For example, if you have a pain, thinking about it may often seem to make it worse. The key is to understand that if you can make your pain worse just by thinking about it, you ought to be able to have the opposite effect on it too, simply by focusing on it. If you have a pain in your shoulder, imagine moving it down your arm, through your wrist and into your hand. Each time you 'move' your pain to a new location, continue to focus on it, until you have moved it right down to your fingertips. Then imagine it seeping slowly out of your fingers until it has completely gone. Another method is to imagine your pain as a colour – perhaps a bright, flaming red. As you focus on it, imagine the colour slowly changing to a duller red, then orange, yellow, green and blue. It finally becomes a soft violet hue. As the colours 'cool', your pain also cools until it disappears or becomes insignificant.

Although your body will probably respond better and more quickly to the images that *you* personally conjure up, you may find some of the following suggestions helpful as a starting point for some of the more common ailments. Most of them have been suggested, and beneficially used over the years, by my patients:

Ailments and healing images

- **Arteries and heart disease.** Water flows freely through a wide, open river. A crew in a small boat all row together, easily and efficiently pulling the slender boat across the smooth water surface.

- **Arthritis.** Someone comes along with an oil can, and the rough edges of the joint start to become smoother.

- **Asthma and lung disease.** Tiny elastic bands that constrict your airways pop open. A vacuum cleaner sucks the mucus from your airways. Waves calmly rise and fall on the ocean surface.

- **Cancer.** The tap that controls the blood supply to the tumour is turned off, and the cancer cells starve. Radiation or chemotherapy enters your body like healing rays of light that destroy cancer cells.

- **Depression.** Your troubles and feelings of sadness are attached to big colourful helium balloons, and are floating off into a clear blue sky. A warm, strong sun breaks through dark clouds. You feel a sense of detachment and lightness, enabling you to float easily through your day.

- **Diabetes.** Small insulin keys unlock doors to hungry cells, and allow nourishing blood sugar in. An alarm goes off and a sleeping pancreas wakes up to the smell of coffee.

- **Cuts and injuries.** Plaster covers a crack in the wall. Cells and fibres stick together with superglue. Jigsaw puzzle pieces come together.

- **Infections.** White blood cells with flashing red sirens arrest and imprison harmful bacteria. An army equipped with powerful antibiotic missiles attacks enemy germs. A hot flame chases bacteria out of your body.

- **Overactive immune system (allergies, asthma, arthritis, etc.)** Hyper-alert immune cells in a fire station are reassured that the allergens have triggered a false alarm, and they can return to playing their game of cards. The civil war ends with warring sides agreeing not to attack their fellow citizens.

- **Stress and tension.** A tight twisted rope slowly untwists. Wax softens and melts. Tension swirls out of your body and into a drain or stream.

- **Weak immune system (immune deficiency disorders: HIV, AIDS, etc.)** Sluggish, sleepy white blood cells awaken, put on protective armour, and enter the fight against the virus. White blood cells rapidly multiply like millions of seeds bursting from a single, ripe seed pod.

Many scientific studies show that focusing your imagination in specific ways can be calming, encouraging, mood-changing, and pain relieving, and may accelerate or allow physical as well as mental healing. It's certainly a better use of your mental energy than imagining all the possible bad things that can happen.

Self-healing

The following self-healing exercise can be used in different ways. As before, you can simply read it as you would any article, with the intention of learning something and discovering how it might help you; alternatively, you may find it useful to read it more deeply several times to yourself, pausing when it comes to breaks identified by a three-point ellipsis (...) in order to have time to experience that section in whatever way feels comfortable to you. Probably most effective is to speak it into a tape recorder (or have someone else read it for you) and then, as you listen to it, close your eyes and follow in whatever way feels right to you. A version of this meditation is available on my CD, *Deep Healing* (see Resources).

Find a quiet place where you can sit and relax comfortably, and take in several slow, deep breaths. As you do so, imagine that you are letting out any conflict. Just unwind, relax and find a peaceful space within yourself. As you breathe in, imagine that you are letting peace come in ...

Imagine a beautiful rainbow, and relax with each breath. As you settle down, let the waves of colour from the rainbow move down through your body, bringing peace and relaxation ...

Imagine now that you are going to a special place that you love, a place that perhaps you hold in your heart, where you have felt relaxed at some time in the past. It might be a favourite place that you've visited on holiday, your grandparents' garden, or a place you have seen in a film. It's not important what environment you choose, as long as you feel at peace.

I'd like you to spend several minutes in this place. You can either see yourself sitting or standing in one spot, or walking – whichever you find the most peaceful. Take in the sounds, smells and views all around you.

Bring your attention to the colours and shapes. . .

If you are outdoors, note the colour of the sky and the shapes of the clouds. See the whole expanse of sky, or grass, or sand, or forest, or water.

Focus now on the smells, aromas and fragrances . . .

Perhaps your favourite flower is in bloom. If you're on the beach, smell the ocean smells or the suntan lotion. Savour the pungent scent of the pine forest. If you are in a familiar location, recall the smells and conjure them up as vividly as you can.

Turn your attention now to the sounds of your scene. Listen to the ocean waves breaking on the beach, the sound of bird calls, the gurgling flow of water across the stones in the stream, or the sound of the wind in the trees . . .

Just listen to the sounds of this wonderful place – a place that is so comfortable and peaceful to you.

Watch all the movement in your scene. Perhaps the clouds are moving across the sky, affecting at times the brightness of the sunlight. Watch the glint of light as it bounces off the water in the stream or the birds sitting in a tree. If you wish, see yourself moving – walking on the sand looking at seashells, running through the grass in the meadow, or climbing from rock to rock across the stream.

Focus on sensations and textures. Feel the warm sand and salty air on your skin and in your hair, the grass tickling your naked feet, or the cool slippery surfaces on the stones in the stream . . . Now touch or pick up some favourite object from your special place. Allow your fingertips to gently explore its surface. Is it smooth or rough? Wet or dry? Warm or cold?

Allow yourself to become totally absorbed in the sensual aspects of these images, all in a place where you feel completely comfortable, at home and at peace. If your sense of peace is interrupted by anxious or disturbing thoughts or images, simply observe them. If at some point you think it is boring or foolish to just sit and watch your breath go in and out, note to yourself that this is only a thought, a judgement that your mind is creating. Simply let it go. Then gently return to the specific sights, smells and sensations that surround you.

Begin to sense that something wonderful is about to happen. Feel the tingling sensation of expecting something good . . . Know the sense of certainty. Everything is right, just as it should be.

Now notice a soft glow of golden light from above . . . It begins to bathe your body. A tingling, shimmering, vibrant energy summons you, energises you, soothes you . . . heals you. You are washed in bright goodness, and draw everything you need to you, almost as if you are a powerful magnet. Good wishes and kind thoughts come. This goodness and healing energy seeps into your body, infusing you with a generous, boundless energy and a sense of well-being . . .

Feel it moving through the layers of your body, deeper and deeper into each and every organ, down into your bones ... Feel it in each and every cell, dissolving any blockages, correcting any imbalances. Enjoy this free-flowing, healthy energy sweeping through your body ... Now you are relaxing ... healing.

You are now capable of directing your thoughts, slowing them down, choosing what you want to be thinking about, rather than letting your mind run its own course ...

For a few minutes, focus now on your own images for healing your particular problem ... Your body remembers how to be well, and savours this feeling of well-being. You feel peaceful and easy in your special place – a healing place – one that is always here.

You know it's a place you can visit at any time to feel this healing energy and peace. When you are ready to return, take a deep breath and exhale fully ... Open your eyes and spend a few moments enjoying this relaxed, healthy, comfortable feeling ...

Using your imagination

Although I have given you a list of suggested images for various illnesses, I usually tell my patients that their own images will probably act more powerfully because they have invested their own creative energies in the process. Some years ago I was told an amusing story by a woman who attended one of my seminars. She had been suffering from an extremely bad back problem that caused such acute pain she was forced to spend a couple of weeks immobile on a hard bed. Ironically, she was a physiotherapist. But as she lay waiting for nature to take its course it occurred to her that visualisation might possibly help her.

As she relaxed and began to imagine her spine, a clear and anatomically precise picture began to form in her mind's eye. She then perceived one disc that appeared to be out of alignment with the others and pressing on a nerve. She was wondering what image she could possibly use to ease the slightly slipped disc back into place when an image spontaneously sprang into her mind and played out like a piece of film. It was so ridiculous that it made her laugh. Coming down her spine was the cartoon figure from the Tetley tea-bag TV commercials, pulling behind him a garden roller. When he approached the injured area of her back, he carefully and gently rolled her spine until the offending disc was 'eased' back into place again. Within a couple of days she was back on her feet and working – pain free. It is not so much a matter of *thinking* of an image, but rather of allowing one to form spontaneously.

Chapter 8

Healing and Creativity

We ought, every day at least, to hear a little song, read a poem, see fine
pictures, and, if it were possible, to speak a few reasonable words.
(Johann Wolfgang von Goethe)

When, in 1990, I bought Sturgeon's Hall – my home and workplace
in Suffolk – one of my first tasks was to decorate what became my
treatment and waiting rooms. I knew that I wanted to use colour
rather than having four white walls in each room, but the question
was which colours to use, as different colours mean different things
to different people. Although blue is recognised as a 'healing' colour
by many people, for me it can also be a cold colour. I always feel
that red is an energising colour but I felt that some of my patients
might associate it, even subconsciously, with pain, blood or anger. I
eventually settled on a deep yellow wallpaper decorated with gold
stars – yellow is neutral yet warm and friendly and, as I was to
discover, children loved the stars. Since then countless people have
come into that room saying, 'What a lovely sunny room.' Sometimes
it has been a dull rainy day outside but the effect has worked –
people feel uplifted.

Shortly before I moved to Sturgeon's Hall, I had been invited by
the oncologist Professor Karol Sikora to give a lecture to his

medical students at the Hammersmith Hospital in London. I had given several talks at hospitals around the country and was always struck by how drab and uninspiring the buildings were. Often painted in shades of grey or cream, they seemed sad and soulless, not only for students but, much more importantly, for the patients being treated within them.

Ten years later I visited the Hammersmith Hospital again and was delighted to see that changes had been made. Now, your fear and anxiety is eased as you walk along a tunnel connecting the main building to the new cancer clinic. Along the tunnel walls are wonderful murals. You find yourself walking down a sandy beach towards a clear blue sea. The scene becomes more surreal as you notice that you are walking through the waves to a point where you are completely submerged. You are surrounded by playful-looking dolphins that benignly and protectively help you along your way. As you leave the Dolphin Tunnel at the other end, you find yourself once again walking up a beach into the entrance of the clinic where you are welcomed into a new state-of-the-art glass building with a high atrium. It works strikingly well as a way of bringing about a sense of light, peace and relaxation, and − most of all − fun, for patients and hospital staff alike.

'Beautiful objects and brilliancy of colour are actual means of recovery,' Florence Nightingale wrote in 1859 in *Notes on Nursing*. One hundred and fifty years later, her ideas are being put into practice in hospitals and medical centres around the world. Angela Clow, Professor of Psychophysiology at Westminster University, is a world authority on the biochemistry of stress. She has made a comparison of the physiological state of patients in a day-surgery waiting room with music and art on the walls, as opposed to one with no music and plain white walls. She found that patients surrounded by art and music had lower heart rates, lower blood pressure and lower levels of the stress hormone cortisol, and needed less sedation before their surgery. Wondering why good feelings or happiness should have such an effect on the immune system, Clow speculated that there is an evolutionary mechanism in operation: our happiest ancestors were bold creatures who socialised and ventured out to explore. This brought them into contact with infection, so they needed higher levels of antibodies in a stronger immune system.

Clow then conducted another innovative study, the results of which were published in 2006. She and her colleagues investigated the physical and emotional effects that a midday visit to the Guildhall Art Gallery in London had on a selection of high-flying City workers. After just 40 minutes of viewing the Guildhall's collection, participants reported a 45 per cent reduction in their perceived stress levels; this was confirmed physiologically by saliva samples registering a 32 per cent drop in levels of cortisol.

The potency of this creative form of stress reduction was verified by the 'above average' levels of stress in participants at the start of the trial and the speed with which they became calm. The workers involved in the trial were found to have higher concentrations of cortisol in their body than is normal in those of a similar age and at that time of day. Following their visit to the gallery, these levels were reduced to a level below that of an average person. The speed at which the levels dropped was striking: in normal circumstances it would take about five hours for stress hormone levels to fall to this extent, and not the 40 minutes experienced by the study participants.

In 1984, Dr Roger Ulrich, director of the Centre for Health Systems and Design at Texas University, conducted what was then a very innovative study of patients recovering from gall bladder surgery. To his surprise, he found that those with views of trees from their hospital windows went home almost a day earlier, used fewer heavy medications, had fewer minor complications such as nausea, and showed better emotional well-being than patients whose windows looked out onto brick walls. In research on patient anxiety in a dental fears clinic, he found that patients felt less stressed when a large mural depicting a natural scene was hung on the wall of the waiting room, in contrast to when the wall was blank.

In another study at a Swedish hospital, Ulrich found that open-heart surgery patients in intensive care units could reduce their anxiety and need for pain-relieving drugs by looking at pictures of trees and water. Patients were randomly assigned a nature picture (dominated either by water or trees), or one of various abstract pictures, or no picture at all (control group). Those exposed to the picture of nature with water experienced less post-operative anxiety than either the patients exposed to other types of pictures or the control group. Patients exposed to abstract pictures had higher anxiety than patients without any picture. After many years of research, he now believes that the most effective images include mainly elements that have been important to humans throughout a million years of evolution: (1) nature elements such as trees, plants, and water; (2) happy, laughing, or caring faces; (3) benign animals such as pets.

These and other findings form the basis of Ulrich's theory of 'supportive design', a series of guidelines for designers of healthcare facilities. To soothe patients, families and employees, he says, buildings should incorporate features such as nature views and nature-related art in patients' rooms, aquariums in waiting areas, atria with greenery and fountains and gardens where patients, family and staff can find relief. As Prince Charles has noted: 'It can't be easy to be healed in a soulless concrete box with characterless windows, inhospitable corridors, and purely functional wards. The spirit needs healing as well as the body.'

In Britain there is now an organisation called the National Network for the Arts in Health which is recognised by the Department of Health. It is active in all types of medical facilities including hospitals, hospices, surgeries, walk-in centres and day care. Its many recent projects have included:

- redesigning the hall and atrium at Middlesbrough Hospital to reduce patient stress and create a physical environment that feels less like a hospital. In the spinal injuries department at the same hospital there is an artist in residence – a poet who will work with patients

- drumming workshops for young patients at Oakham House Hospital in Leicester

- painting, drawing, collage, papier mâché, ceramics and mosaics being offered to patients through health centres in Carlisle and outlying villages

- provision of small pamphlets of poetry suitable to read while patients are waiting to see their doctor

- a commission to make a contemporary handwoven tapestry and two paintings for the Accident and Emergency Department of Homerton Hospital in London

Art and healing

In today's world we tend to leave art in the realm of the decorator or the fine artist. Decorators and designers, like Roger Ulrich, use art to add colour and mood to a space. Museums, galleries and private collectors buy art to record the cultural identities of society. People seeing art in these settings receive a vision of the artist's perception of the world that can create a wonderful connection, enabling them to identify with someone else's experience of the world. Before Western civilisation turned art into a commodity, its purpose was for honouring the spirits of the universe and healing the body and soul. Art moved us beyond our fears of the unknown, allowing us to integrate our life experiences in order to live fully and in harmony with the earth. Today, we are not so different from our ancestors. Stress over our fears disconnects us from our source – the endless well of inspiration that only our imagination can tap. Too difficult to define, we leave the imagination to those few who seem to be 'born' with it.

However, you don't have to be an artist to access the images that lie within, waiting to heal your life. All you need is the willingness to remain open to the process and the ability to suspend judgement. You don't need to be artistic – you don't have to be good at drawing, painting, mixing colours or anything creative. You merely have to try to express yourself using paper, paint, clay, chalk or crayons. It provides a wonderful, tactile way to release emotions and convey feelings.

Having a serious illness or disability is traumatic for everyone and sometimes my patients have found it easier to paint or draw their feelings rather than talk about them. This is borne out by an increasing number of reports published in medical journals. For example, a project at a Philadelphia hospital showed a 47 per cent decrease in anxiety and 38 per cent decrease in depression for cancer patients who participated in art therapy.

As well as providing an opportunity to explore your deeper feelings about yourself and others, the benefits of creating art include:

• relaxation and stress reduction

• expression to connect with your feelings

• using your imagination to transform pain

• a heightened sense of empowerment and well-being

• processing grief and trauma

- a focus to provide a sense of purpose

- documenting your experience

A study published in the *Journal of Pain and Symptom Management* in 2006 found that introducing art therapy to patients can reduce a broad spectrum of symptoms, including those related to pain and anxiety in cancer sufferers. In the study, conducted at the Northwestern Memorial Hospital in Chicago, researcher Dr Judith Paice wanted to see if the creative process involved in making art really is healing and life-enhancing. Fifty patients from the in-patient oncology unit of the hospital were enrolled in the study over a four-month period. They all reported significant reductions in eight of nine symptoms measured by the Edmonton Symptom Assessment Scale (ESAS) after spending an hour working on arts projects of their choice. The ESAS is a numeric scale allowing patients to assess their symptoms of pain, tiredness, nausea, depression, anxiety, drowsiness, lack of appetite and well-being and shortness of breath. Nausea was the only symptom that did not change as a result of the art therapy sessions.

Numerous studies like these show that art heals by changing your physiology and attitude. The body's physiological state changes from one of stress to one of deep relaxation, from one of fear to one of creativity and inspiration. Art affects your autonomic nervous system, your hormonal balance and your brain neurotransmitters. It immediately changes your perceptions of your world, as well as changing attitude, emotional state and pain perception. It creates hope and positivity, helping you to cope with difficulties. It can transform your outlook and way of being in the world. But, of course, creativity is not limited solely to art: it encompasses many other areas including writing, music and gardening – all of which can be valuable healing tools.

Joe's story

Joe Bidder was 47 years old when, in 1985, he began to suffer from a neurological condition which was eventually diagnosed as multi-system atrophy. He was suffering from loss of balance, unsteadiness, uneven walking and the inability to run or jump. He started to suffer considerable pain in both legs at all times of the day and night. His left arm and hand lost half of their use and his speech was occasionally slurring. In the autumn of 1988, neurologists told him that he might have just five years to live. It was at this point that he first came to me for healing.

By February of the following year he had become much more positive about his future and decided to work seriously towards publishing a collection of poetry. As he started to write, his condition began to stabilise and he later described 1989 as his 'first year of transformation'. In addition to the healing sessions he had with me, Joe had weekly counselling sessions with a psychotherapist who said very little.

> I talked and finally worked through my fears of death and dying a horrible death. I was able to transform these sessions into some powerful poetry. Once the fear of death had been banished, a huge surge of energy was released and my life became productive and rewarding. I became a *warrior* and shed my prior persona as *victim*.

In 1990 he published a collection of poetry, *Matter of Life and Death*, and shortly afterwards co-founded Survivors Poetry – a national literature organisation funded by the Arts Council of England which eventually comprised some 30 poetry groups across Britain organising 1,500 events a year. As well as becoming chair of the Arts Council of England Disability Advisory Panel, he was asked to become an advisor and consultant to the Arts Council.

Writing poetry became one of the most important healing tools that Joe discovered, leading to fulfilment in other areas of his life too. Contrary to the gloomy predictions of his neurologist in 1988, he is still visiting me and writing poetry in 2006 – almost 20 years later. The same principle applies to writing as to art: you don't need to be a great writer – you merely have to try to express your feelings using words. As with art, it can provide a wonderful way to release emotions that can lead to a healing path.

Writing and healing

In a study published in 2005 in the *Proceedings of the National Academy of Sciences*, researchers in America reported that asthma sufferers can have an attack on hearing a stressful word such as 'wheeze'. They used brain scanning to show for the first time a direct link between brain activity and the worsening of symptoms such as breathlessness. When an asthma sufferer is exposed to emotionally charged words about their condition, it activates brain regions that can trigger inflammation. This aggravates breathing difficulties. Doctors and sufferers have long suspected that stress and emotional turmoil can set off inflammatory symptoms in asthma.

In the study, volunteers were asked to inhale ragweed or dust-mite extracts likely to affect their condition. They were then shown three types of words which were either asthma-related – including words such as 'wheeze' – or negative but unrelated words such as 'loneliness', or neutral words, like 'curtains'. Brain scans revealed that the asthma-related terms lit up two brain regions – the anterior cingulate cortex (which appears to play a role in regulating heart rate and blood pressure and is vital to cognitive functions such as decision-making, empathy and emotion) and the insula (which is believed to process feelings of unease, fear, disgust and pain) – and were strongly linked to measures of worsening lung function and increasing inflammation. The negative words that were unrelated to asthma produced no reaction in the brain. Professor Richard Davidson, who led the research, said the two brain structures affected were involved in controlling the physiological condition of the body, such as shortness of breath and pain levels. In asthmatics these two areas of the brain 'may be responsive to emotional and physiological signals, like inflammation, which may in turn influence the severity of symptoms,' he said.

However, while certain words can *trigger* an asthma attack, using words in a different way can actually *reduce* symptoms. In 1999, the *Journal of the American Medical Association* reported that writing about stressful life events helped to reduce symptoms of asthma and rheumatoid arthritis in patients with these illnesses. The effects of the writing exercise were still evident four months later. These findings added to a growing body of evidence linking mental health to physical well-being. Researchers are still not quite sure how this technique – called 'expressive writing' or 'journalling' – can lead to improvements in health. On average, asthma patients who wrote about their most stressful life event showed a 19 per cent improvement in a specific measure of lung function, while control asthma patients showed no change, the researchers reported. Rheumatoid arthritis patients were found to have a 28 per cent reduction in symptoms, whereas control group arthritis patients did not improve.

Ventilation of negative emotion, even just to an unknown reader, seems to have helped these patients acknowledge, bear, and put into perspective their distress. If the authors of this study had provided similar evidence about a new drug, it would almost certainly be in widespread use within a short time!

Journalling is an ancient tradition dating back to at least the tenth century in Japan, when 'Pillow Books' were used to record daily lives and thoughts. Yet it is only now being rediscovered – although the term 'journalling' is usually used to refer to personal writing that explores the inner world of the self. Recent studies completed by scientists at various universities have proven that this form of writing contributes directly to your physical health. Tests conducted by teams of clinical psychologists and immunologists have demonstrated that subjects who wrote thoughtfully and emotionally about traumatic experiences achieved the following results:

- increased T-cell production

- a reduction in visits to the doctor

- fewer days off work

- generally improved physical health

- quicker healing of wounds among people who wrote about their troubles as opposed to those who wrote about frivolous things

You don't need any special tools or abilities to start expressive writing, and since it is for your use only, spelling, handwriting and grammar are not important. The purpose of writing is for you to get your feelings and experiences down on paper. Two techniques that will get you started are 'cathartic writing' and 'unsent letters'.

Cathartic writing

Write about all your feelings. Put your pain, fear, anger, frustrations and grief down on paper. Say what you want to say, need to say, on the page. The journal won't judge or criticise you. You can use it as a safe place to let out everything you feel. Sometimes you might choose to throw away your writing, or burn it as a rite of releasing the event or feeling that is disrupting your life. Let your intuition lead you in your writing, and in what you do with the words once you've written them. Also try writing when you're feeling really happy. Begin with the phrase, 'Right now I feel ...'. Then let yourself write whatever comes out. If you run out of feelings, reread what you've just written and then write the next thing that comes to mind. Write for at least 20 minutes, at least once a day for a week, without stopping or pondering. Just write whatever comes into your mind and you will be pleasantly surprised how you quickly get into writing about what is troubling you.

Unsent letters

You can write a letter to a person, place, event, or belief. This gives you a powerful way to express what you experience and feel about any situation. Your writing will give you a place to express your true feelings when you may not feel comfortable doing it more directly. This technique is especially helpful in dealing with death or divorce. These are situations where you may not be able to talk to the person directly. It is also a powerful way to process the emotions that come up in a relationship. Start the letter by writing, 'Dear . . .'. Then let your pen and paper lead you. You may be surprised at the power and clarity you experience from your writing and may find it a starting point for a whole new level of communication with others.

Normally, you will notice improvement in the condition you are writing about within a few days. Begin journalling and start to also experience these benefits:

- **Clarify your thoughts and feelings.** Do you ever seem completely jumbled-up inside, unsure of what you want or feel? Taking a few minutes to jot down your thoughts and emotions will quickly get you in touch with your internal world.

- **Know yourself better.** By writing routinely, you will get to know what makes you feel happy and confident. You'll also become clear about situations and people who may not be good for you.

- **Reduce stress.** Writing about anger, guilt and other painful emotions helps to release the intensity of these feelings. By doing so you will feel calmer and better able to stay in the present.

- **Solve problems more effectively.** Usually we solve problems from a left-brained, logical, rational perspective. Sometimes the answer can be better found by engaging right-brained creativity and intuition. Writing helps to unlock these capabilities and gives you the chance to find unexpected solutions for what seemed insoluble problems.

- **Resolve disagreements with others.** Writing about misunderstandings rather than bottling them up will help you to understand someone else's point of view. You may then see a sensible resolution to the conflict.

Music and healing

We all have a connection with music. Our tastes may be different, but still, music has a way of touching us all. It is a universal language that transcends words. Music can support our feelings, it can motivate us to be active and, conversely, it can soothe and relax us. It seems to reach people when other things don't, perhaps because it is associated with important events in our life. Music can offer an outlet for stress, help us express our thoughts and emotions through song. More than anything music can uplift our spirits.

Throughout my life as a healer, music has been a crucial ingredient of my work. It makes a world of difference to the healing experience, softening the atmosphere and enhancing patients' receptivity to energies. It can also inspire hope, optimism and a fighting spirit. I deliberately choose descriptive music that will hopefully conjure up visual images and transport my patients to the far reaches of their imagination. I also use music in my work to fix an association with the healing experience, enabling my patients to revisit that experience whenever they like. Many of them buy a copy of the music I've played because they find that when they later play it at home it can prolong the benefits of the healing. This effect now seems to be borne out by recent research.

Dr Ardesh Kumar, research associate professor in the Department of Psychiatry and Behavioural Sciences at the University of Miami, has studied the healing effects of music on several neurohormones and neurotransmitters. Research results have shown that levels of melatonin increased significantly after listening to music. Melatonin, which has a relaxing and healing effect, helps regulate sleep and is secreted mostly at night. Six weeks after the study, melatonin levels almost doubled.

I am always careful to choose music that my patients are unlikely to have heard in another connection because a piece of music, like a perfume, can have very powerful emotions attached to it. Although there are numerous well-known pieces of music that I find positive and uplifting, I tend to avoid them when healing because they may bring up painful memories or associations in someone else.

Researchers in London are now carrying out a study to see if music could be introduced on the NHS to help patients with dementia. Scientists at Imperial College in London are studying music therapy to see if they can prove that it has long-term benefits for dementia sufferers. The therapy involves professional musicians and patients playing instruments and making music to bring about physical, mental, emotional and spiritual changes. While the benefits of music have been known for thousands of years, much of the evidence has been anecdotal. However, numerous recent studies examining the effects of music therapy confirm that listening to music really does have an impact on health.

- At California State University, studies showed that chronic migraine patients who started and continued to listen regularly to their favourite music reported 83 per cent fewer headaches.

- At St Agnes Hospital in Baltimore, patients in critical care units listen to classical music. 'Half an hour of music produced the same effect as ten milligrams of Valium,' reports Dr Ramond Bahr, director of the coronary care unit.

- Listening to music has been found to reduce mood disturbance in cancer patients undergoing stem cell transplantation, a procedure known to cause significant psychological distress. Other data suggests that music may alleviate anxiety in patients undergoing radiotherapy treatment, and that it improves the quality of life in people with terminal cancer.

- In another trial, women undergoing colposcopy reported reduced anxiety and pain perception after listening to slow, rhythmic music.

- Premature babies at UCLA in Los Angeles and at Georgia Baptist Medical Center in Atlanta gained weight faster and used oxygen more efficiently when music was being played in the neonatal unit. At the Tallahassee Memorial Regional Medical Center, babies have shorter stays in the intensive care unit when music is played for them daily, compared to babies in control groups without music.

- Researchers from Michigan State University reported in 1999 that group keyboard lessons given to older people reduced stress, loneliness and anxiety, while increasing levels of human growth hormone. This hormone is implicated in such ageing phenomena as osteoporosis, energy levels, wrinkling, muscle mass, and aches and pains.

• In 2000, another team of researchers reported that a particular type of group drumming activity appears to boost the function of natural killer cells that seek out and destroy cancer cells and virally infected cells in our bodies.

Most of us choose to listen to music we 'like', but this may not always give the best results for healing. Often, the music we are least attracted to will have the greatest benefit. If you are angry, your first instinct is to put on some really angry music. Does it help, or does it perpetuate how you feel? Alternatively, if you play some light and happy music, by comparison to how you are feeling it may make you feel angrier. Selecting the right music to listen to is not always so simple.

Choose a piece of music that matches your current mood. Now try arranging a series of different musical pieces in sequence, gradually approaching the mood you want to move to. For example, if you are dealing with depression, choose a composition that to you represents depression in its extreme form. Follow this with one that is only mildly depressing, then select a neutral piece, and end with music that is clearly uplifting and motivating. Listening to music in a sequence like this will allow your current stress level or mood to be first acknowledged and then gradually transformed.

Try to find time to sit down, relax and listen to the musical piece all the way through, without interruption and without doing anything else. This allows for the optimum response to the transformation process. We all have a tendency to use music as a background to other activities. Try developing the technique of just listening to the music. This way you will get the greatest benefit from it.

It is through your response to the music that emotional memories, or inspirations, can be released. Don't think that you have to stay still and concentrate on the music. If it inspires you to get up and do something, or if your mind begins to wander, that is fine. Allow yourself to experience all your responses without judgement. On the other hand, do not start listening to the music while you are already engaged in other unrelated activities. The important thing is to let the music embrace you totally.

Allow it to reach your inner feelings, and respond freely to it. You may experience visual images, thoughts, movement, an intensification of emotion, physical vibrations, sleep – or nothing at all. When the music has finished, bask in the silence for a while as this will help integrate your feelings.

Gardening and healing

Diana had suffered from rheumatoid arthritis for over 20 years. When I met her, she had been told that she would be wheelchair-bound, if not bedridden, before too long. As if this wasn't enough, she had also been diagnosed with Sjogren's syndrome, which leads to the body having an inability to produce moisture – in her case particularly in her mouth and upper respiratory tubes. This made eating virtually impossible and at times she was unable to swallow. When Diana first came for healing there was doubt as to whether she was strong enough to travel from her home in Wales; she had recently been hospitalised on three occasions and each time her life had been under threat.

Five years later, although she still has health problems, her life is quite different. Not only has she travelled as far afield as Costa Rica, she has also created an extraordinary garden – 'Grandma's Garden' – that is now open to the public. One recent visitor reported, 'We even met Grandma who is an inspiration. She was buzzing around the grounds in her wheelchair making sure the new pond was being properly constructed!' It was a far cry from her previous situation. However, I don't feel that it is all attributable to her healing sessions with me – a large part has also been the driving creative force that has led her to create a remarkable garden. She explains:

> I'd never been a gardener, but I know what I like and where I want to put it. The whole of the estate incorporates the use of the senses, with an emphasis on the use of sight, sound, smell, taste and touch. Listen to the wind as it rustles through the trees, the grasses, the quivering foliage of plants and seed. Hear and see the insects attracted to the strong colours of the flowers. Smell the aromatic flowers and wild plants. The herb garden is full of tasty plants used in flavourings in cooking and concoctions such as herb tea. Last but not least of the senses is touch. Plants use different textured leaves to protect them from the elements and from attack by pests. Touch some of the plants with your eyes closed and you will instantly understand the importance of the sense of touch.

Diana also explains how the garden, from its earliest concept, became a creative project on many different levels:

> I found, having applied for a grant, that plans had to be drawn up, forms filled in, meetings attended and deadlines met. This necessitated a creative way of allocating, not so much time, as energy in order to fulfil all these requirements. But the advantage of all this was that I met new people, new ideas, new environments, new ways of looking at things, examining other people's ideas and suggestions to combine or reject. All this had the effect of stimulating and enhancing my own creative process.
>
> A major effect of this is that while the mind is occupied with so many new, exciting and challenging things, there is little time left for sitting in a huddle contemplating the pain, the impairment, the tiredness and the unfairness of life.
>
> The only way to overcome illness or physical impairment is to learn,

for at least some of the time, to be creative for creation's sake – not for necessity or financial gain. When we access this way of thinking and being, a new potential for healing opens up.

By most people's standards, I am not healed – but that raises the question of what is healing? By many standards, including the medical profession, I should not still be alive. In fact, I am alive and kicking – albeit within my limits of kickability! There are days when I am unable to overcome the effects of illness and disability but those days are spent in what I consider to be my 'consolidation days'. Time out to be spent allowing the body to do its own thing – to recharge and to relax knowing that I love it enough to listen to it when it needs to be heard. These days are spent daydreaming, often becoming highly involved in the creative process of a project and its outcome on a mental level.

Diana and I share a passion for gardens and gardening – it is where much of my creative energy is directed and I have always felt that there is a close link between gardening and healing. Gardens can give us a sense of control, important when we often feel that there are so many things beyond our control. I know that I can't control nature, but at least in my garden I can exercise some choice in deciding what to grow, when and where. There are so many things to tap into in a garden that contribute to our well-being and health. As Diana discovered, a garden allows us to indulge our senses, and sensory stimulation is crucial to healthy human functioning. In fact, the sensory element is fundamental to the garden's appeal: feeling the surprisingly velvety petal of a poppy or the roughness of tree bark; inhaling the sweet scent of a rose; tasting a freshly picked tomato; hearing the rustle of grasses and the birdsong; seeing the infinite range of colours in a tree peony.

Jean, another of my patients who has been battling cancer for many years, has also discovered the healing pull of the garden:

Whereas I had previously considered deadheading merely a job that *had* to be done, it became a task that took on a new meaning. The feel of the warm soil in my hands, the sun on my back, and the fresh smells of the earth and flowers after a gentle shower, produced a period of renewal in my life. Instead of worrying what the doctors would say on the next visit, I pored over seed catalogues, making plans about which seeds and bulbs I would order and where I would plant them. The garden became my goal. It became a healing garden.

I also like to think of my garden as being a healing garden, and I love showing people around it. When I bought Sturgeon's Hall, it took me two years just to clear brambles, undergrowth, thistles and nettles. Now, except in the most inclement weather, it is also enjoyed by my patients – either as they look out onto it during our healing sessions, or as they sit relaxing in it afterwards.

Chapter 9

Healing and Relationships

After a while you learn the subtle difference between holding a hand and chaining a soul. And you learn that love doesn't mean leaning and company doesn't always mean security. (Veronica A. Shoffstall)

Health is not just the absence of diseases or illness. Health is defined as a state of complete physical, mental and social well-being, a definition which incorporates the importance of social support and close personal relationships. In 1988, Dr James House published in the prestigious journal *Science* what was then a landmark paper. Entitled 'Social relationships and health', it reviewed half a dozen studies of a total of over 22,000 men and women and found that people without well-established support systems had significantly shorter life expectancies than those with good and varied personal networks. Those with few friends and acquaintances and without good supportive relationships had a death rate *two to four times higher* than those with extensive networks. His conclusion was startling: a lack of social relationships is a major risk factor for health – rivalling the effects of well-established pathological risk factors including smoking, obesity and high blood pressure.

One of the most interesting recent findings is that women with strong support systems may be less likely to develop fatal cancer.

Researchers Dr Peggy Reynolds and Dr George Kaplan of the University of California followed almost 7,000 people for over 17 years. Women with the fewest social contacts were more than twice as likely to die of cancer as those with a large number of social connections. For reasons that are not clear, socially isolated women were particularly prone to hormone-related cancer, including breast cancer.

However, as I will explain later in the chapter, people who may choose to be socially isolated sometimes redress the balance by preferring the company of a pet. I remember once watching a television documentary on the work of the Blue Cross Animal Hospital in London. An elderly woman with a shopping trolley containing four Pekinese dogs was asked by the interviewer why she had four, and weren't they a lot to look after? Her vehement reply was that they were 'her life'. She explained that she had rescued them when she heard they were to be put down by a neighbour who was moving abroad and could not take them with her. Looking after them had given her, she said, something to get up for each day, something to care for. 'I saved their life,' she said, 'and they saved mine.'

Recent research focusing on the connection between relationships with others and physical health also tells us that:

- An unhappy marriage increases the chances of becoming ill by 35 per cent and can shorten one's life by an average of four years.

- Children growing up in unstable marriages tend to have higher levels of stress, causing them to be sick more often.

Certain relationship characteristics protect us against physical disease and illness, such as:

- being close and connected

- being able to solve problems and make decisions as a team

- being able to cope with a variety of situations together

- being able to talk honestly and openly

Lack of social support and close relationships has been linked with physical conditions such as heart disease, different forms of cancer, epilepsy, inflammatory bowel disease and arthritis. The quality of personal relationships has also been linked to the physical health of the elderly, the immune system, reproductive health, smoking and drinking habits, and risk-taking behaviour. The following are some examples:

- Couples who are more negative or hostile while discussing marital problems have more negative changes in their immune system up to 24 hours after their discussion.

- Children who come from divorced families are more likely to start smoking, and males from divorced families are more likely to be problem drinkers.

- People who are grieving the loss of a loved one are more likely to use alcohol and tranquillisers.

Relationships and women's health

Researchers have discovered that long-term anger and hostility between partners is much more dangerous for women than men and can impair the immune system. In a study published in 2005 in the *Archives of General Psychiatry*, Dr Janice Kiecolt-Glaser and her colleagues at Ohio State University recruited 42 healthy couples who had been married an average of 12 years to spend two 24-hour periods in a hospital research unit. On the first visit, the couples were encouraged to be loving and supportive of each other. On the second visit, they talked about their areas of marital conflict. On each visit, a special vacuum tube created blister wounds on their arms that were monitored for healing. The most antagonistic couples took an average of a day longer to heal. The researchers found that hostile marital interactions increased the production of stress hormones more for women than for men.

This is possibly because women remember both positive and negative interactions more than men. Women are generally more aware of the emotional content of a relationship. They tend to have larger and broader social networks than men, and they are more sensitive to 'adverse events' in those networks – a friend, a child or a sister in trouble. That sensitivity is especially acute when it comes to their most intimate relationship, with their husband or partner.

Long-term unhappy marriages can have serious health consequences. In a new study published in 2005 in the *Archives of Internal Medicine*, researchers looked at data from 400 healthy women who were followed for 13 years before and after the menopause. They found that marital dissatisfaction tripled a woman's chances of metabolic syndrome, a group of heart-risk factors. Only widows were more likely to have metabolic syndrome than the unhappy wives; even divorced and single women had better health-risk profiles. In other words, a bad relationship can hurt a woman's heart in more ways than one. Unhappiness at home may even be fatal after a heart attack. A Swedish study published in the *Journal of the American Medical Association* in 2000 found that women with coronary heart disease had a greater risk of recurrence if they had severe stress in their marriages or live-in relationships. The researchers said that emotional strain and lack of support from a partner may mean that a woman is less likely to stay with heart-healthy behaviour and may not seek essential medical care. On the other hand, stress at work did not appear to affect the health of women who worked outside the home.

Several other studies have also shown that good marriages help to keep women healthy. It is not just the absence of relationship stress, although that is certainly a factor. Women in happy marriages have strong social support, which generally encourages healthier behaviour. In fact, researchers have found that women in positive relationships actually benefit from spending more time with their partners. This has now been labelled 'intimacy inoculation', and is known to be able to protect us from disease.

Dr Kiecolt-Glaser says couples should learn to keep hostility in check. When relationships are stressed, she says, you see a kind of 'tit for tat' behaviour where events can really escalate. The most important thing is to cut that off at an early stage. All couples argue, but it is the quality of the disagreement that matters. If you find yourself reaching an impasse with your partner, you could say, 'We really see this quite differently,' rather than, 'You idiot! How could you *possibly* think that?'

Emotional hunger

If you deprive yourself of food and water for long enough, you will drastically damage your health and will eventually die. Yet so many people seem oblivious to the equal danger of what amounts to an 'emotional hunger strike'. Throughout your life you receive what psychologists call 'strokes' from those around you. A stroke is a form of recognition or stimulation that arouses feelings – either positively or negatively. A positive stroke is a compliment from someone else, a kind word, or a smile. A negative stroke would be someone else's hurtful words, a cold stare, or a reprimand. In reality, whether people are unpleasant or charming to you, you are being stroked. It is a confirmation that you exist and is essential for survival. If you are not successful in getting your needs met in positive, life-affirming ways, you may find yourself looking for them in negative, illness-inducing ways rather than being ignored.

Strokes also create feelings and emotions within you. If someone pays you an unexpected compliment it will probably leave you happy and cheerful for the rest of the day. If someone puts you down, it may depress you for hours. Because of the way we are brought up as children these emotional responses tend to become classified as 'good' or 'bad'. For example, smiling passive behaviour is rewarded in children whereas displays of fear, anger or sadness are often punished. This leads to suppression or dulling of our emotions. We lose trust in our own experience. I believe that this running away from or burying our emotions can contribute to ill-health in later life.

You have the ability to choose a more positive path instead of potentially self-destructive attitudes. If you project your past experiences of pain into your future, you will spend the rest of your life haunted by fear. Fear of emotions, mistakes, success, failure, other people, yourself, weakness or rejection by others. You might not be able to change past events but you can change your thoughts, emotions and attitudes towards them. That, for me, is often where true healing starts.

People everywhere are looking for love, feeling sad and rejected if they don't get it. The trouble is that most people are looking for love to come from outside themselves. If as a child you felt loved, you are more likely to feel comfortable expressing your feelings. However, if you felt unloved, you may well feel threatened and fearful about expressing your innermost feelings and, for protection, will bottle them up. Furthermore, if you perceive that one of your parents didn't love you, in your childlike mind you assume responsibility for this condition by condemning yourself as being unlovable. To compensate for this perceived lack of love, you may try to earn love from your parents and peers by pleasing them – a strategy which then gets projected onto all your other relationships. Your ability to love can only come from within *you*. The best way to put more love into your life is to start giving love, and the best place to start is by learning to love yourself.

Loving kindness, loving awareness

There is a traditional Buddhist meditational practice known as 'Loving Kindness, Loving Awareness', that I have often used in my workshops. Its purpose is to help you experience different aspects of love: love for oneself, and for friends and enemies alike. It is a simple exercise that you can easily practise yourself. Find a comfortable position in which to sit, and close your eyes. You can either record this meditation onto a tape yourself, or ask a friend to read it for you.

1. Focus and experience loving yourself. Look at yourself and bring into mind 'Love' and what it means in relation to your own self. Be aware of any associated feelings, impressions, associations, images — maybe even colours.

2. Focus on love for someone to whom you already feel a close bond. How does love appear in this situation? Again, note any associated feelings or ideas.

3. Take as an object of your love a 'neutral' person, someone towards whom you have no particularly strong feelings one way or another. Once again, note any associated ideas or feelings.

4. Focus now on someone to whom you have very negative feelings — someone you really dislike — and extend the same feelings of love to them.

5. Now bring all of these people together and extend the same feelings of love towards them all.

Achieving healthy relationships

As we have seen, there is abundant medical literature linking effective immune response to supportive relationships. We need both intimacy and community to boost our immune systems. In other words, a good relationship is an immune booster. The following factors all have a vital contribution to make to achieving good relationships:

Hard work

Perhaps the easiest part is getting married or being born into a family. The real work involves staying married and maintaining closeness with your family members. Couples who stay together need social support. This can come from family or friends. Family reunions or 'get-togethers' tie us together. Knowing and understanding each other's relatives helps couples to connect in deeper ways. You are more likely to learn about family history – and family quirks! Connecting with friends can do the same, especially if your friends share your values.

Consistency

Intimacy is how well you feel understood, accepted, appreciated, cared for and loved by the significant people in your life. They must also feel mutually understood. What does it take to achieve this? Consistency is a key factor that helps couples in relationships. Consistency in areas such as kindness, giving, sharing thoughts and feelings, building trust, and displaying love and affection, will strengthen and deepen your love in a relationship. Consider each of these areas and evaluate how you are doing with each of them. If you feel you aren't doing too well, *work at being better and more consistent.*

Commitment

This is the foundation of a solid relationship. It is 'being there' when needed – and anticipating the need. You need to encourage growth in your partner and have a willingness to work at deepening the relationship. We are all imperfect and have faults. The couple that is truly committed has developed a friendship, and will deal with problems accordingly. The love must be strong enough to endure, and the good must outweigh the bad. This results in a strong, solid foundation.

Trust

This is being able to count on each other and know that only your best interests will be considered by the other. It is being able to share your deepest feelings, fears, hopes and secrets – knowing that these will be handled with care. *The ultimate test of trust comes when you know that you can trust your life with someone else.*

Separateness

Too much separateness leads to isolation, but too little can be smothering. Each person must develop individual interests and activities to enrich the time spent together. Men and women are different and it's best to retain your own likes and dislikes. But, show respect for your partner's interests and the time allocated for them to spend with friends. Always respect each other's belief systems because no two people think exactly the same way.

Communication

Partners need to be able to share a wide range of feelings. Hurts, fears, anger and inadequacies, as well as joy, hopes and dreams, can be difficult to share. Intimacy will grow as you share your vulnerabilities and offer understanding in return. Listening without criticism is probably one of the hardest skills to master, but it is also one of the most important. Try to listen to what your partner is saying without jumping in and criticising. Just listen, accept, and try to understand your partner's point of view. It's also important to learn to say you're sorry, even if it's not always easy to do.

Playfulness

A sense of humour and playfulness add joy and relieve tension in any relationship. Try spontaneity, silliness and surprise. Laughter is the best medicine. The couple who laugh together, stay together. Keep humour in your home and don't take life too seriously. You might as well make it fun.

Time

You must spend time together and make time for each other a priority in your lives. It is impossible for strangers to be intimate. It takes time for intimacy to develop. Spending time with your partner or spouse is the best way to demonstrate that you value the relationship. Time together allows you to build good memories and a 'bank' of shared experiences to sustain the relationship.

Relationships and illness

If you are lucky, you might go through life relatively unscathed by illness – whether yours or that of someone close to you. Many people are not so lucky and all too soon become familiar with the exhaustion, heartbreak and disappointment that illness can bring. In this situation illness can take a great toll on relationships with those closest to the ill person. The relationship, whether it is parent–child, partner, sibling or whoever, will be at risk of losing its original focus and becoming lost in the illness. In the course of my work, I am accustomed to watching the breakdown of some of my patients' marriages and relationships. It is probably not so much that illness deals a fatal blow to the marriage but that the relationship was on shaky ground prior to the illness, which then exacerbates the problems. If a relationship has been troubled, then people have a much harder time because they don't have a history of love and friendship to cushion the illness. What happens in any crisis is that either the relationship becomes strengthened as you grow and become strengthened, or it falls apart.

But chronic illness doesn't have to be a prescription for marital misery. Most of my patients and their partners learn to cope successfully with their new situations, and some even come to feel the disease brings them closer, forcing them to re-examine their relationship and mend any weak spots. Relationships become stronger invariably because those involved have realised that love can grow 'in sickness and in health', if they both commit to sharing their feelings (no matter how hard that may be) and both learn to adapt as circumstances change.

You may find that your illness is not initially accepted or understood. You may even have trouble in convincing others that you have a serious problem that imposes major restrictions on you. 'But you look so well,' or 'Just pull yourself together and snap out of it,' are the sort of comments you don't want to hear. Like some of my patients, you may well find yourself on the end of well-intentioned but unsolicited advice. Getting others to understand and accept your situation may be a major problem. Your condition may create problems within the family. Having less energy makes it difficult to do as much as before and both you and other family members may have difficulty adjusting expectations to new limits. Family members may have to assume new responsibilities, which can sometimes create resentment. You might feel guilty about not doing your share, and your limitations may make you uncomfortably dependent on others. You may also find that the unpredictability of symptoms can make it difficult to maintain existing relationships outside the family. Being ill makes it harder to get together with people, and you may find that you are unable to socialise in the way that you used to. Having less energy, while at the same time worrying about being accepted, it's easy to be discouraged from the effort of establishing new relationships.

You may find that your restrictions feed fears about being abandoned. If you find that you don't have your former energy, you may fear that you will lose the ability to take care of yourself or that those on whom you depend may leave you. On top of all this, feeling ill and being dependent makes it much more difficult to be assertive than it was before. Sometimes you adopt others' expectations for yourself as your own and make your situation more difficult by pushing yourself too far. Assertiveness means setting safe limits for yourself, then communicating them to others:

- Make clear to yourself and to others the consequences of your efforts to meet old expectations: they may intensify your symptoms and delay improvement.

- Be as specific as possible in asking for help if others offer it. It can be difficult to be assertive if you feel dependent and are fearful of being abandoned.

- If that is the case for you, it may help to practise saying your request to yourself or someone you trust before making it to the person whose help you want. In presenting your request, it may help to acknowledge that you understand the other person's situation. You might say something like, 'I know my illness makes your life more difficult and that some things I say and do may be frustrating . . .'

Looking for the good

Many people find that the sudden onset of illness is very similar to a sense of bereavement. The diagnosis of a serious or chronic illness is often the start of a journey which will be punctuated by loss and change. Your losses may include health, privacy, control, role identity, independence, means of productivity or self-fulfilment, self-image, dreams or goals for the future, relationships, feeling good, undisturbed sleep, play or recreational activities, and energy, among many others.

'An illness or a disability – I know this is true for me – prevents one from living life as one has always lived it. In other words, we have to start again, to learn to grieve for the person we once were and accept the person we have become or are becoming,' says Diana, a patient of mine. 'Once this difficult process has been gone through then we can become open to our new talents, however simple we perceive these to be.'

Once you have got over the initial feeling of shock and disbelief, you may experience immense anger. There may also be feelings of guilt or regret over what has not been done or achieved in earlier years. You may feel you have to deal with these emotions by yourself, leading to feelings of isolation and resentment. Grief is a large part of the journey through any illness. This journey involves not only the person who is ill, but also their friends, family and anyone close to them. So many hopes and dreams can be lost. When someone becomes ill over a protracted or indeterminate length of time, family and friends too can be thrown into a process of grieving. This can be characterised initially by shock, denial, anger and depression. Grieving is normal, and should not be suppressed. Whether you are the person who is ill or someone close to them, not expressing grief, and not having it acknowledged by someone else, can result in bottled-up feelings that can really damage a relationship.

A high proportion of my patients have found it very important to have friends in whom they can confide their anxiety, fear, and sometimes anger. However, it is just as important to be able to share the positive feelings of joy, hope, optimism and excitement. If you can only share the negative feelings, your relationships can become unhappy. Friendships based only on bad news are as stilted as friendships based exclusively on good news. In all your intimate relationships, you ought to be able to express a full range of emotions. While this may not always be possible, it is nevertheless a good goal to aspire to.

Dr George F. Solomon, one of the pioneering researchers of mind–body medicine, says that many of us have wonderful friends and families, but we remain lonely or isolated because we don't turn to them. We keep them at arm's length, not wanting to bother them about our pains and problems, saying, 'I don't want to upset them,' or 'They have enough with their own problems and I'll only add to their burden.'

Research suggests that relationships are more stable if there is an emphasis on the positive, so look for the good in one another and the relationship. A study charting the amount of time that couples spent fighting versus the time they spent interacting positively (touching, smiling, paying compliments, laughing, etc.) found that relations were stable and satisfying if the ratio of positive interaction to negative was five to one.

Dealing with negative feelings

Again, there is a very effective exercise which can help you to release and transmute negative feelings from within a relationship. You will need to involve a friend for this exercise. Sit opposite one another, making direct eye contact, but avoiding verbal communication.

1.   Look at your partner and imagine that he or she really likes you. He or she thinks you are a kind, loving person and is really happy to be with you. Be aware of any thoughts, feelings, images or physical reactions that occur, and examine them.

2.   Imagine that your partner really dislikes you. He or she is criticising you and looking at you with scorn and hate. Examine what you feel and think now.

3.   Imagine your partner is someone from whom you can learn. See him or her as being an instrument in your growth. Examine how that feels.

4.   Imagine the partner to be another soul, a human being, a source of unconditional love, someone whom you can accept without condition and vice versa.

At the end of the exercise, discuss with your partner your reactions and feelings to each part of the exercise. Examine, experience and learn from each other how it felt to be sitting with someone who either loved or disliked you.

'News and goods'

Another simple exercise called 'News and goods' is particularly effective for helping you to focus on the positives in your everyday life. 'News and goods' is a simple antidote to creeping negativity in intimate relationships.

1.   *Think about your typical day, and try to assess how much of what happens in that day (and your resulting mood state) is positive, negative or neutral. Although it will vary considerably from one day to another, most people will say that 70 per cent is neutral, 15 per cent is negative, and 15 per cent is positive. What do you focus on most with your partner when you are at home together? If your answer is not the negative, you are in the minority.*

2.   *When your partner comes home (or you come home), ask him or her: 'What new and good thing happened to you today?' Then he or she asks you the same question. What if nothing good seems to have happened? Try looking deeper into your day, holding onto small moments of delight. Something new and good might be an amazing sunset you saw on your way home, or a flower that has blossomed in the garden. There is* always *something, no matter how small, that can give you moments of delight and pleasure.*

Improving communication

Illness, especially when it is serious, affects all aspects of relationships and communication becomes especially important. Lack of communication can lead to isolation, frustration and unmet needs. People with illness who don't discuss it often feel that they are facing things alone. Talking about and sharing emotions and needs allows couples, families and friends to work together to resolve problems and face difficult situations. If you leave your feelings and wishes unsaid, it is easy to be left with inaccurate, even hurtful assumptions about why the people who care about you are behaving in a particular way. Sharing your sadness and fears also lets those around you know how much you care for and love them. Discussing feelings and problems with honesty, sincerity and openness can greatly reduce the stress that illness places on relationships.

Working to improve communication is another way to help increase understanding, uncover unrealistic expectations, and aid cooperative problem solving. You can't expect your spouse or partner to read your mind. Here are some suggestions to help improve communication with your partner:

1. **Pick a good time.** Choose a time for important conversations when both you and your partner will be at their best. Find a time when you will not be distracted by pain or 'brain-fog', and when your partner can give you their full attention.

2. **Be grateful and respectful.** Treat your partner with respect, acknowledging their support and effort. Avoid demeaning comments, sarcasm and blaming. Like abuse, criticism can sometimes be about power. Acknowledge your part in family problems.

3. **Practise problem solving.** Focus on the difficulties caused by the illness, rather than personalising problems. Think of 'gripes and solutions': describe complaints, and then discuss possible solutions. Work on only one or two problems at a time. Try not to use generalisations like 'I need you to love me', but instead describe specific actions such as 'I need you to hug me when I come home'. Stated this way, your needs help to set boundaries and, if agreed to, become the 'rules' of the relationship.

4. **Test your understanding.** From time to time, check whether you have understood the other person's position by restating it in your own words.

The role of the caregiver

When someone becomes ill and cannot do some of the things for themselves that they once did, those close by can become unwillingly drawn into the position of caregiver. Some people adapt, some don't. If you are the sort of caregiver who tends to seek rescue projects, caring for a loved one who is chronically ill may burn you out. If you don't want to be a caregiver but force yourself to do it out of guilt or obligation, you may also become burned out. The last thing someone who is ill needs is your resentment. Even if you are a willing caregiver, you must share the burden of care, whatever it is. Invite others to be a part of this (which may be easier said than done), and take time off to get support for yourself, enjoy social time, and feel good about yourself. You need to be constantly renewed in order to constantly give.

It is important that the person who is ill is aware that their caregiver is in a difficult position too. The illness also affects them. Let them get the support they need, encourage them to get it when they are not seeking it, don't make totally unreasonable demands, and if at all possible, try to involve caregivers whose caregiving is coming from a healthy and truly caring place. If the burden of care is damaging your relationship, get help. Healing is harder to find when your primary relationships are not working.

Relationships and pets

Of course, not all of my patients are married or have a partner, yet this need not mean that they are any less likely to heal. Some people prefer the company of their beloved dog or cat. This relationship can also bring rewards, not least in relieving stress and loneliness. Pets provide us with companionship and an emotional relationship. Some of my patients who have lost a cherished pet are as upset as if they had lost a dear human friend. Research suggests that pets can buffer our reactions to acute stress as well as reducing our perception of stress. They are also seen as non-judgemental.

Over the past 15 years, scientists the world over have established beyond doubt the therapeutic value of animal companions. In Cambridge, researchers found that within a month of taking a new cat or dog into their home, owners reported a 'highly significant' reduction in minor ailments. The Baker Medical Research Institute in Melbourne, Australia, showed that the health benefits were even more far-reaching. A study of some 6,000 patients revealed that those with pets had lower blood pressure, lower cholesterol levels and, as a result, a reduced risk of heart attack. American researchers have established that, even after a heart attack, pet owners are more likely than other coronary patients to be alive a year later. A Japanese Animal Hospital Association study of people over 65 found that pet owners made up to 30 per cent fewer visits to doctors than those who had no pet.

The reasons are simple: pets help to reduce our state of arousal, which reduces blood pressure. We are fulfilling our most primitive and basic need – the need to touch. They can also help by making us feel less lonely, by creating a feeling of being needed and by encouraging social contact with others interested in animals. They are a stimulus for healthy exercise, they keep us busy and make us feel safe. We all crave affection, but sometimes we find we have difficulty obtaining it from other people. A study at Warwick University found that people who were poor at confiding in others, showing love, or making friends, were able to lavish affection on a pet. Pets – or companion animals – provide friendship, constancy and love. They're always there, always happy to see us.

In Britain, some prisons now encourage inmates to keep pets — birds, tropical fish, even cats. These can be a magical ingredient to bring about long-term changes in attitude and behaviour, with prisoners often discovering for the first time what it's like to give and receive affection.

Pet owners often feel needed and responsible, which may stimulate the survival incentive. They feel they need to survive to take care of their pets. (Many cancer patients with pets have lived longer because they felt their pets needed them.) Stroking a dog, watching a kitten tumble, or watching the hypnotic movements of fish can be an antidote to a bad mood or a tiring day. Pets can shift our narrow focus beyond ourselves, helping us to feel connected to a larger world.

Illness is not an easy experience for anyone, and nor are relationships. Yet relationships with another human being may be one of the greatest gifts we ever have. When a relationship is tested by illness, the level of commitment to another human being is tested, and all are challenged to work on a relationship that exists within new parameters. There is no guarantee when we commit to any type of relationship with another person that it will work out in a predictable or easy way, but each of us is fully deserving of being in fulfilling relationships with others. Sometimes the relationships we most want don't survive an illness, and it is the unexpected ones that grow to be the relationships that count. Illness has a way of separating out those who are able to really be there for us, and those who aren't. However, with work, and by seeking various supports, healthy, challenging and enriching relationships can be enabled to flourish within the context of illness.

All too frequently in our busy lives we don't take time to nurture relationships. We need to connect with others on a deeper level. True intimacy replenishes our souls. Most of us have experienced a magical moment in which everything seemed perfect. You may have had that moment while praying. You may have felt it while holding your sleeping newborn child, or when you yourself were held in a warm embrace by someone who loves you. You may have felt it when listening to music, creating a work of art, labouring on a project you truly believe in, or while on a walk through the countryside.

These are moments of oneness with creation, times when every cell in your body resonates with a sense of rightness, when every fibre of your being says life is good. These moments restore us spiritually and recharge us emotionally. They also do wonders for us physically, reinvigorating and replenishing our immune system and making us feel more vital and alive.

Sigmund Freud once said that 'In the final analysis, we must love in order not to fall ill.' Lack of love is, I am sure, a root cause of much illness. What Freud advocated all those years ago has now been demonstrated scientifically through the results of many medical researchers whose work I have drawn on throughout this book. A recurrent theme throughout most of Aldous Huxley's life was that 'One never loves enough.' In a lecture shortly before he died in 1963, he said, 'It is a little embarrassing that, after forty-five years of research and study, the best advice I can give to people is to be a little kinder to each other.' That is the best advice I, too, could probably give – but with an addendum:

Be a little kinder to each other – and to yourself.

Resources

For further information about Matthew's healing practice, workshops, books, and CDs (including some of the exercises in this book) please visit www.matthewmanning.com or call 0870 8500570.

Organisations

Ainsworth's Homeopathic Chemist
36 New Cavendish Street
London
W1G 8UF
Tel: 020 7935 5330

Association of Hypnotists and Psychotherapists
12 Cross Street
Nelson
Lancashire
BB9 7EN
Tel: 01282 699378

British Association for Counselling (BAC)
1 Regent Place
Rugby
Warwickshire
CV21 2PY
Tel: 01788 578328
Website: www.bacp.co.uk

British Medical Acupuncture Society
67–69 Chancery Lane
London
WC2A 1AF
Website: www.medical-acupuncture.co.uk

The British Wheel of Yoga
25 Jermyn Street
Sleaford
Lincolnshire
NG34 7RU
Tel: 01529 306851
Fax: 01529 303233
Email: office@bwy.org.uk
Website: www.bwy.org.uk

Hypnotherapist
Dr Brian Roet
2 The Mews
6 Putney Common
London
SW15 1HL
Tel: 020 8780 2284

The Institute for Optimum Nutrition
Blades Court
Deodor Road
London
SW15 2NU
Tel: 020 8877 9993
Email: allion@ion.ac.uk
Website: www.optimumnutrition.co.uk

The National Federation of Spiritual Healers
Old Manor Farm Studio
Church Street
Sunbury-on-Thames
Middlesex
TW6 6RG
Tel: 01932 783164
Fax: 01932 779648
Email: office@nfsh.org.uk

Penny Brohn Cancer Care (formerly Bristol Cancer Help Centre)
Chapel Pill Lane
Pill
Bristol
BS20 0HH
Tel: 01275 370100
Email: info@pennybrohn.org
Website: www.pennybrohncancercare.org

Support Services

BACUP (British Association of Cancer United Patients)
(Information, counselling, leaflets and research information)
3 Bath Place
Rivington Street
London
EC2A 3YR
Tel: 020 7613 2121

Cancerlink
7 Britannia Street
London
WC1X 9YN
Tel: 020 7833 2451
Young people's line: 0800 591028
Website: www.cancerlink.org

The Compassionate Friends
(Self-help group of parents who have lost a child of any age)
53 North Street
Bristol
BS3 1EN
Tel: 0117 953 9639
Website: www.tcf.org.uk

Cruse
(Bereavement counselling)
126 Sheen Road
Richmond
TW9 1UR
Tel: 020 8332 7227
Website: www.crusebereavementcare.org.uk

National Cancer Alliance
PO Box 579
Oxford
OX4 1LB
Tel: 01685 793566
Website: www.nationalcanceralliance.co.uk

Index